THE MOST HATED AND
UNWANTED CHILD

THE MOST HATED AND UNWANTED CHILD

By

Jenifer Stewart, BA, CSPDT

ISBN: 978-0-578-88911-5 (paperback)

PROLOGUE

If you ain't ready for the ride, then get the hell out of the car!
Life is about choices and timeless thoughts! This story is about
a child who has perished due to the lack of love and affection
from an exceedingly rare set of insidious, vile, and callous cohabitants. She has a mother who is jealous of her child and
has always had a thirst to be in her child's shoes. Her thirst is
so bad it drives her to do the unthinkable! When things don't
go her way, she is on a path beyond destruction. Her father is
so callous his tongue would cut glass.

DEDICATION

In memory of Nicholas Charron Ceasar. When you born, I felt as though you brought out the best in me by making me a woman. On the other hand, when you were taken from me, there were no words to describe the pain. I must say the loss of you has brought the best out of me! I love you son! My first husband and knight in shining armor! Continue to rest easy.

Nicholas Charron Ceasar: August 29,
1989–Sept. 30, 2020

In honor of Emmitt Reese (aka Pappy). You were the grandfather I never truly had; you were a mentor to me as well. You *always, always, always* told me I need to write a book about my life! Continue to rest easy, Emmitt Reese—October 23, 1924–November 18, 2014. I love and miss you dearly!

PREFACE

They prevented me in the day of my calamity: but the Lord was my stay. He brought me forth also into a large place; he delivered me, because he delighted in me.

Psalm 18:18–19

This book was written on the strength of me holding onto a lot of traumatic experiences and painful memories with my parents. Over my lifetime, there have been a lot of untold truths about me stemming from my parents. The situations and issues I endured during my life are unforgettable, implausible experiences, which are unacceptable and much more than any one individual should ever encounter.

The pain of the loss of my first son is unexplainable. I felt as though I would explode sleeping just one hour a night for months. My mind would not stop racing for half a second. I prayed to God to help me! I asked God, "Why am I still waking up every day?" I told God, "You shouldn't allow anyone to live through this sort of pain!" My heart would ache like a toothache; touching my chest area over my heart would be painful.

God showed me 90 percent of the pressure inside me was the traumatic experiences with my parents. I could never make them proud in any way; none of my dreams or goals were perfect enough. Instead, I had seven beautiful, amazing, and unique men who admired me with all their hearts and souls. I've lost three of my men to God's battle! Neither of my parents have ever been there for me through these painful times, showing me not even a nanometer of love or care. Instead, they delivered more pain and agony to my life. My spirit said, "This is where you start. You write, you release; let go of them and don't look back!"

CHAPTER 1

It does not matter about the amount of ice in the glass; cream always floats to the top. Just as the sun sets, it will rise again.
—Jenifer Stewart

(1972–2010)

ON OCTOBER 11, 1972, a beautiful 8 lb. 8 oz. baby girl was born. My name was Rhonda Anissa Fairley for the first three days of my life. It was on the third day that my name was changed to Jenifer Fairley prior to being discharged from Womack Army Hospital with my mother Laverne. My name was changed for the final time once Laverne and Lucas were married and switched their last name to Downing. Laverne and Lucas divorced when I was eight months old. The first time my name was changed from Rhonda Anissa to Jenifer because Margaret and Grace wanted a granddaughter and niece with the name Jenifer.

Lucas, with his authoritative self, decided to rename me again to Jenifer Downing, not wanting me to carry his father's last name, Fairley. He instead gave me his brother's father's last name, Downing. I was well loved as a baby by my family members and their friends. The family would pass me around from lap to lap, bouncing me up and down on their laps, saying, "Boom"; this is how I got my nickname "Boomie." I was such an intelligent little girl that during my kindergarten year at Lucille Sounders Elementary School in Fayetteville, NC, I was moved up to the first grade. I went to summer school and took eleventh grade English and math in order to skip the eleventh grade.

I graduated at sixteen years old and had dreams of becoming an airline stewardess, model, or photographer. Laverne and Lucas pulled me in so many directions I eventually lost myself. Margaret had ideas of what she wanted to see her granddaughter become as well. The sad thing is no one ever focused on me and what I wanted to become. Through it all, I loved my cohabitants with all my heart and soul, and I admired them both. All I ever wanted was to receive genuine love.

My cohabitants are insidious, vile, and callous. Laverne spoiled me as a child. On the other hand, I was in this dark hole my entire childhood and adulthood because Laverne mentally abused me. I was so unhappy and lonely as a child that I tried to commit suicide on more than one occasion. The sadness was too much for me to handle; I went to mental health counseling for years, trying to cope with my life. Laverne has always been and will be a wolf in sheep's clothing.

It was mortifying how I would beg to go live with Lucas, who was no better; at least mentally I would've had peace of mind. I often wondered why they had me. Laverne tormented Lucas's wife badly for years, which is the main reason I could never go live with Lucas. My stepmother was so distraught and drained from Laverne's behavior for years she had no energy or mental compacity to deal with Laverne's vile actions. She would call all hours of the night, saying obnoxious things to my stepmother when she answered the phone.

I remember a time when she called and my stepmother answered. Laverne said to her, "Why the hell are you always answering the phone? Let Lucas answer the phone sometimes." It was incidents like this that caused me to suffer and live a miserable childhood. There was only one thing I ever wanted in life, and that was to sit down and have dinner with my mother and father. I longed so bad for that experience. Neither Laverne nor Lucas would ever come to that agreement to fulfill my one special wish, which has laid inside me my entire life.

They wouldn't give me that one moment together; it's sad since they had sexual intercourse for many, many years but couldn't give their one and only daughter that special moment. Laverne had a boyfriend named Bean who would come over sometimes when she would allow him. Bean's job would have him out of town on the weekends sometimes. He was a good man toward Laverne and me. I would always say to him, "Bean, why don't you and my mom have a baby?"

He would say, "You have to talk to you momma about that. Maybe you can change her mind." On the weekends, Bean had to work out of town; Lucas was creeping!

No one can imagine the pain and hurt I felt when she told me she was pregnant with my little brother. Laverne boasted all the time about how she was almost five months pregnant with my little brother when she had an abortion. Yes! It was Lucas's son! I remember begging Laverne to have me a little brother so I would not be lonely. She always told me, "No! now go somewhere and leave me alone!" She never agreed or

3

considered it; instead she agreed to have sexual encounters with Lucas long after they were divorced for countless years.

Lucas had a key to Laverne's house for years. When we lived in Rosehill Gardens apartments, Lucas and Laverne would make a pallet on the floor at the foot of Laverne's bed and put me on it. They would have sex all night, then Lucas would get up and leave the next morning, going back home to his wife in SC at the time. Keep in mind the sex went on for years, ending in 2008. It was all well and fine; I eventually got the brother I'd always wanted from Lucas and my stepmother.

I love my brother deeply; he's my sweetheart. The love I have for him is enormous; no one would ever know the difference. My childhood years were rough. Even though I received everything I wanted, I still was not happy. For me, I didn't get to experience a lot of things normal children did.

The only way I got to attend a football game was when I would go to Aunt Grace or Aunt Frances's house on the weekends. I felt so deprived of living the life of a young teen in my middle school years. I would ask Laverne, "Can I go to the game after school?" Her response was "No, only whores and bitches go to games after school." Laverne did sign me up for pageants, of course; that's what she wanted for me. That was ok. It was a privilege for me to be allowed to go skating with my friends on skate nights. My cousin Gail signed me up with Seabrook Recreation Center where I became a Seabrook Majorette.

I was in a lot of parades with the bands; those were the times I felt at large and was in touch with myself mentally. Twirling the baton was my thing, and I was so excited and ready. During practice, the room echoed as we marched in place with our white boots and attached red pom poms swinging from side to side as we twirled around. Dropping low doing our cheers, the sound would have my heart racing, but when I twirled that baton in my hand and opened the palm of my hand and let it spin for me to see the reflection from the light in the ceiling sparkle on my baton, I felt unlatched. On the day of parades, sometimes it would be so cold I would think, *I can't perform.*

We started marching from downtown; when we got in front of Fayetteville State University, I saw my Aunt Grace. She would always be on the sidewalk in front of Fayetteville State University in the same location where all the bands would break it down. She would be yelling, "Break it down, Boomie Tyme. It's your time!" Aunt Grace would tell me all the time, "I don't see how you function, Boomie Tyme, between your mother, father, and grandmother. They are always pulling you in different directions about what to do with your life." She would get so upset and say, "They are messing you up mentally, and they don't even realize it." She said, "I've tried to talk to your grandmother and Lucas about how they need to stop pulling you in different directions." She said, "It does no good."

One thing my Aunt Grace told me on multiple occasions is "It's your life, you do what's going to make you happy. Do what you choose to do. You become who you want to become, not what they want you to become!" Everything I would share with Laverne about any of my accomplishments or goals, she would always downgrade them. She tried her best to discourage me from anything my heart desired. She never wanted to see me excel. The only thing she attempted to do was allow me to go to modeling school, which didn't last long. The school was called Shantel Models, located on Green St. in downtown Fayetteville, NC.

She enrolled me in the school, and as I started to excel, companies begin to reach out to Shantel Models in reference to me. I had opportunities to go to Wilmington, NC, and Los Angeles, CA, and *boom* she drops the bomb! "I'm going to take you out of Shantel Models. I can't afford to keep paying $100 month anymore!"

I told her, "Call Lucas, he will pay! I don't want to stop my modeling classes!"

So she did; the first thing he inquired about were my grades. Lucas stated, "She needs to be making straight As."

Laverne said, "She has As and Bs and one C."

Laverne's boyfriend Bean said, "Leave her in modeling school, I'll pay for it."

She said, "No!" I'm taking her out!"

Bean then said, "Laverne, that don't make no sense how mean you are! That's the only child you have, and you don't her right." He continued, "Yeah! You buy her all the clothes and shoes she wants. You put her clothes in cleaners when I put mine in there. She is making good grades in school, at least let her do want she wants sometimes. You got her in all kinds of pageants; that's what you want her to do! She wants to become a model, she is doing well, and they are calling for her."

Laverne took me out anyway. Well, that was one of my dreams gone out the window.

The more things were going off the track, the more I would start going to Grandmother Margaret's house on the weekends and through the week. My best friend at the time would stay some weekends with me. We would sometimes walk to McDonalds, which was behind the neighborhood. It was a Saturday; the sun was shining bright, the neighbors were out washing their cars, and the neighborhood children were riding their bicycles. It was a beautiful day in Foxfire! I asked my grandmother if we could walk up to McDonalds. She said, "Go 'head. You two be careful out there."

We said, "Ok, we will, Grama!"

No one could tell us we weren't hot stuff that day when we stepped out. We had on gray and white striped shirts with gray miniskirts and white Keds. We always dressed alike. As we were walking into Mc Donald's, two gentleman pulled up into the parking lot; they had on army uniforms. Of course, they approached us. Wilson was short with a butterscotch complexion and a boxed haircut. He asked me my name, I told him, and we exchanged numbers; we talked on the phone a lot and spent time together on the weekends and through the week.

I finally introduced him to Laverne. He started coming by the house more and more. Sometimes she would be there other times she was at work. If he came while Bean was there, he still would have to be gone by a certain time. Sometimes I would slip him in the window. As time went on, Laverne and Bean would have disagreements, and she would put him out of the house. During this time, she started seeing a married man named Paul.

He would come on the weekends; for a while, Laverne would have his Jack Daniels and Sprite with an ice bucket by the bed and two crystal glasses. The doorbell would ring, and I would just go in my room, close my door, and turn my music up to drown out the sounds of lovemaking I preferred not to hear. One weekend, he couldn't make his appointment with her, and she was Louisiana Tabasco hot! Sometimes Wilson would come see me while Paul was there seeing Laverne. It was this one weekend Paul couldn't make it again, and she called his wife and told her, "Keep your husband home, I'm tired of screwing him!" and slammed the phone down. Wilson was there with me; I was six months pregnant with my Nicholas and tired, so I went to take a nap. I awoke from my nap; I heard moaning and groaning coming from her bedroom.

Truthfully, I thought it was Paul, so I looked outside to see if his car was outside, and it wasn't. Wilson's car was the only vehicle outside, so I put a mirror under the door and saw her having sex with my husband. I was sixteen at the time, and I really thought I was dreaming or I was seeing things. I went back into the room and lay across the bed while my unborn child kicked me to no end; he could feel the distress and pain inside my womb. No matter which way I lay on the bed, Nicholas kept kicking and kicking.

Wilson eventually came in the room. I asked him, "Where are you coming from?"

He said, "The store."

I said, "You a damn lie! I know what the hell I just seen!"

He said, "What are you talking about, Jenifer?"

I said, "You were in there having sex with Laverne!"

He said, "No! It wasn't me; I was at the store. That was Paul."

I was hurt so bad and shocked that a mother could do a daughter that way. It was then when my eyes should've been opened to the real world.

I gave birth to Nicholas a few months later and moved to Louisiana when he was one year old. I later returned to North Carolina when things were not working out between Wilson and me. We eventually divorced because of his infidelities. He had a wandering dick! Everyone is aware of life being like a box of chocolates; you never know what you're going to bite into. I eventually met someone else, and things started to get serious. He was my world, my chocolate Buck! The next thing you know, I had a little chocolate bunny that weighed 2 lbs. 3/4 oz.

The second day of Traveon's life, he had to be airlifted to NUC Chapel Hill for emergency surgery. Cross Creek Hospital called Margaret's house to inform me of the situation. Then the phone rang again as Margaret was on her way out the door looking sociably sophisticated as she always does. We both pick up the phone at the same time; I stayed silent when I heard her voice. Margaret said, "Hello!"

It was Laverne; Margaret told her Cape Fear Valley Hospital just called and said, "They are airlifting Traveon to NUC Chapel Hill for emergency surgery. He has a hole in his intestines from being born early; his intestines were not fully developed."

Laverne responded, "I hope he dies in surgery; she don't need him."

This was the first day my grandmother told me Laverne had a bad vendetta against me and I needed to watch out for her. As time went on, things would just happen, and Laverne was the cause and reason for a lot of it. Laverne even went to the extent of calling my grandmother and telling her, "Vengeance is mine. You will pay." Then there was the time she mailed my grandmother a note, which read, "Vengeance is mine. You will pay," and the note had a white powdery substance inside it. I was sitting at the table when my grandmother opened it. She said, "This isn't nobody but Laverne trying to work her roots and witchcraft on me. I'm not thinking about her and her foolishness. My God is almighty!"

My grandmother had a longtime boyfriend of forty plus

years in her life. I stopped by his house to see him as I usually did. This day was so shiny and bright, but I was not feeling as good as the outside looked.

Pappy said, "Hey, Boomie, come on in and sit down! What's wrong, honey, it's such a pretty day outside, and you look so sad. Come on and talk to ole pap. You can talk to me about anything, and you know that."

I said, "I know, Pappy, I'm still trying to find my grandfather, and I can't. No one will tell me anything at all!"

He said, "Honey, you are going through so much with your mother, and you're always being pulled in different directions; they hold secrets from you. I'm going help you all I can!" He gets up and goes to fix himself some Crown Royal in a glass on two rocks and grabs a private stock beer out the refrigerator. He then goes on to say, "Let me fix us some whipta whoptees" (little sausages wrapped in a biscuit with bacon around it). He puts them in the oven, comes over to table, takes a sip of his drink, and said, "You don't even know who you are, do you?

I said, "Why do you say that, Pappy?" It was in this engrossing conversation with Pappy that I found out I was not who I had believed I was all those years.

He said, "Look at me and listen to me good, ok! Do you know that when you were born you were named Rhonda Anissa Fairley? Jenifer Downing is not your name at all. Downing is your uncle's father's last name, not your father's last name. They changed your name several times."

I said, "*What!*"

He continued, "Yes, they did, and I'm not shitting you! Get up and ride with me, I'll show you. Come on, let's go!"

I said, "Let me get the food out the oven."

He took me to Cumberland County Courthouse; we went

to the birth certificate area. All the books were stack up and spread out on the counters. I said, "Wow! Pappy, you can just come in here and look at these records like this?"

He said, "Yes, you can." He looked up Rhonda Anissa Fairley, and there it was: my birth name crossed out and changed to Jenifer Fairley. Pappy then looks up Jenifer Fairley to show me it was changed again. Fairley was crossed out and now read Jenifer Downing. He said, "Look, you see? They crossed out Fairley and wrote Downing."

Pappy then goes over the marriage licenses to show me where Laverne and Lucas were married as Fairley, and it too was marked out later and changed to Downing. I was obliged for him telling me the truth about this part of my life. This was an important part of my life that I needed to be aware of, and to be honest, if he hadn't told me I would never know. I'd been saying to myself, *I really don't know who I am. I can't find my grandfather.*

The thoughts that entered my head were so significant; I would have extremely bad headaches. I would get the telephone book and call all the Fairleys listed, hoping to find something but only getting my heart broken again. I asked myself so many times how people can live their lives not knowing who their families are or, for that matter, not wanting to know. On the other hand, when children are involved, they should be entitled to know. This, too, was another major issue in my life; I was deprived of knowing who my grandfather was. I knew at this point, my grandfather might not be alive anymore.

I had to keep this blocked out of my mind and just accept the fact I would never know him or that side of my real family, for that matter. It just hurt to know that every day I was out and about in the world, I was more than likely looking and walking past a lot of my family members and don't even know them. For me to know he could still be alive and not have any contact with him was a lot for me to handle. I asked Lucas again about my grandfather, and he told me, "The man don't exist and stop going around trying to find him and asking questions."

So I called Pappy and asked him about my grandfather. He told me, "He was a tall brown-skinned man with a star tattooed on his forehead, and he was stationed at Fort Bragg." He tried to help me as much as could, but we had no success. Lucas worked on his family tree for years, and I know he found his father. But he would never tell me. Lucas told me on more than one occasion I would never amount to anything.

Chapter 2

It does not matter about the amount of ice in the glass; cream always floats to the top. Just as the sun sets, it will rise again.
–Jenifer Stewart

(1972–2010)

BONNIE DOONE WAS a hot spot for fun and action; from every side road to the main road Bragg Blvd., it was popping! My Aunt Frances stayed in the place to be for many years. I had a great deal of enjoyable moments at my Aunt Frances's house; I was unbounded when I was there. My cousins and our friends would shoot dice on the back steps, playing for quarters. The weather would always be so right, the wind blowing perfectly enough to keep the sweat off our foreheads. We would sometimes walk to the washerette and shoot pool.

On the way back, we would stop by Hardee's and grab a hot ham and cheese sandwich to hold us over until my Aunt Frances cooked. My favorite dish she would cook was fried lamb chops with sweet peas and corn mixed with her creamy macaroni and cheese and her famous dirt cake. I never could figure out how she got those Oreo cookies and gummy worms to look like they were really coming out of the dirt. I can promise you it did not taste like it looked. Sad, to say, I would have to return home to the evildoer.

The following weekend, I would go back to my Aunt France's house. Aunt Frances said, "Come walk with me to the pawn shop, Jenifer."

I said "Ok!" When I entered the pawn shop, it was the same two older guys that had been there for years; they were both ex-military. Thomas said to Frances, "Hey, how can I help you today?" She proceeded to conduct her business. While she was doing that, I walked up and down aisles looking at the jewelry and the guns.

When she was finished, she said, "I'm ready, Jenifer!" As I walked to the door, I turned around and looked at Thomas in the eyes. He said, "Girl, you got the biggest pretty eyes I've ever seen."

I said, "Thank you."

Then he said, "If you were only of age."

My response was "Don't worry, I will be one day, and you won't be able to afford me. I'll have you driving cabs on the side for extra money."

We both laughed, and Aunt Frances and I walked out into the bright sunny day. Aunt Frances said, "Let's go the washer-ette and play Miss Pac Man!" We stopped by the cleaners on the way and got change for $10. Miss Pac Man was me and my Aunt Frances's sport; we mastered it, meaning we played it until it started over at the first board. The time came when I was of age; Thomas and I spent a lot of time together. We got to know one another and developed an understanding that outsiders could never understand or tolerate. The understanding we had and our views of dating others was one of a kind.

All Thomas wanted was respect. He told me, "Look, JC, you are a beautiful young lady, and I'm not able to satisfy you sexually."

I said, "Ok, and what that supposed to mean? We still can be friends. I like your friendship!"

That was it; I did not care who I met or came across; after that, I told them about Thomas, and if they couldn't accept him, I couldn't deal with them, period. I would give him rides home every day. We would take the boys to the zoo, and we went shopping out of town a lot. He would then spend nights at the house during the week and on the weekends; it depended on what I or he had planned.

Thomas was a godfather/sugar daddy to me; he treated me like a queen and gave me the world. There was nothing in life we wouldn't do for each other. Our relationship blossomed and went on for years until the day he died. I debated so long about introducing him to Laverne. One day, I called my Aunt Frances and mentioned it to her.

She said, "I wouldn't do that if I was you, Jenifer, you know how your mother is." After a few years, I made the biggest mistake of my life by not listening to Aunt Frances. I introduced Laverne to him, and the next thing I knew, he was telling me how she called the pawn shop every day, making conversation.

Laverne even stopped by the pawn shop to see him when she would leave from my house going back to Clinton. There was nothing Thomas withheld from me. She was shuffling her way in slowly but surely. I was living in Devon Wood at the time. One day, I was lying in my waterbed chilling when my phone rang, I missed the call as the phone was ringing. I was turning the cooler on the bed it was a hot muggy day. I had just gotten in from dropping the kids off on my bus route.

It was Thomas on the answering machine. He said, "Hey, JC, call me back as soon as you get this."

I called him back and said, "What's up, Forte?"

He said, "Your mom can suck a mean dick, JC. She put it on me; she can suck a golf ball through a water hose."

I said, "Well, I see you did! You got the life sucked out of your damn dick, so that is obvious! Why did you go over there anyway?"

He said, "Well, baby, she called me at work and said she needed me to bring her some stuff from the store. Ok, being the nice guy that I am, I did. When I got there, she had all these candles and roses everywhere; she even had strawberries with chocolate."

Thomas said he asked her, "Wait a minute, what's going on here? Next thing I know she was going down in my britches. Baby, she just took over me."

Laverne told everyone, "I took her man. Thomas was never her man." She told uncompelling lies to my uncles, and people were upset with me, believing the lies she was telling. One the day, she mailed me a short note, telling me she would see me dead before she sees me with Thomas. She told me I didn't deserve him. She was leaving the same messages on my house phone as well.

Laverne did everything in her almighty power to destroy my relationship with Thomas. Thomas had taken me to the car lot on Raeford Rd. and told me to look around and see what I liked. I saw the new Honda Odyssey Van I had seen in the commercial. The vans had just come on the lot the same day.

I told Thomas, "I like this van." I test drove it, and he purchased it just like that. Laverne eventually got inside his head in the worse way. The next thing I know, Thomas called me and told me to bring him the van and the keys; he was turning the van into the dealership. At this point, I had already had the van a little over a year. She was telling him I didn't love him and all sorts of untruths.

Thomas would call and call and call about me bringing him the van and the keys. I called him and told him to meet me at the Kangaroo on Bragg Blvd. I called my cousin's girlfriend, and she followed me in my other car. After I put the keys in his hand, I ran and jumped in my car and tried to run him over. My cousin's girlfriend was laughing so hard at me; it was too hilarious. With all this going on, I had just found out I was three months pregnant with my fourth son, who would soon be my third living son. Laverne would constantly call the house leaving disturbing messages on my voicemail and sending death threats by mail. She really expected me to leave Thomas alone, but I wouldn't; he had been my friend for years.

She stressed me out to no end. I was on bed rest for several months, trying to control heavy bleeding. Laverne knew I was pregnant; she was trying to make me have a miscarriage. During this time, my cousin Ann and her girlfriend were living with me. My cousin Gail from Lucas's side of the family was also in the Devon Wood neighborhood. Gail and I were the ones who initially moved into the house. The day we picked up the U-Haul on Bragg Blvd., Gail said, "Oh! Shit! Boomie, you going to be driving Mrs. Daisy!"

The U-Haul was a stick shift, and as I drove, switching the gears, Gail said, "Go 'head, Boomie, you are driving Mrs. Daisy!" Gail was the light of my life! We moved all the furniture into the house, and things were flowing well. Laverne started calling and leaving nasty messages on the phone telling everyone to get out of her daughter's house now. At the time, Laverne left the message on the phone. Gail was in the mirror plucking her eyebrows as always; she laughed and said, "Boomie, your mother is crazy! What's wrong with her? This is your house, and I'm not going anywhere."

I told her, "Don't pay her no mind; she tries to rule anybody around me." As a daughter, I always gave her a key to my house in case she needed something while I was at work, and she had the kids or something. Well, she took it upon herself to come in my house while no one was there and throw their stuff outside in the trash and on the ground. Ann had just received her associates degree in recreation from FTCC; she had put that in the trash with Ann's belongings. This was the first time I called the police and filed a report on her.

I called Ann, her girlfriend, and Gail and told them to come home as soon as they could. Things had gotten entirely out of hand; Laverne was continuously tormenting us like it was a hobby for her. She came in our place and demolished our personal belongings. I figured it would be a good idea if I informed Lucas about what was happening. That was the worst mistake I could have made. I called told him I was pregnant, on bedrest, and Laverne was stressing me out to no end and that she would come in the house while no one was home and throw out all their belongings, including Ann's degrees she had just received.

His response was "You need to have and abortion, Jenifer, and I'm taking you out of my will. You don't need to have any more children. Don't call me for anything. I won't ever help or assist you ever."

I said to him, "That's not why I called you in the first place."

Lucas said, "You're sounding just like your mother."

I said, "I won't bother you again."

I was so tired of the treatment I was getting from them; I began to vent to my cousins and told them, no matter what, I couldn't let the way Laverne and Lucas treated me stop me from reaching my goals. The words they would say were just rasping; no matter what, they were not proud of anything I did. I felt I was a on a roll with my life. I was living in Devon Wood, which was a good neighborhood, had two automobiles with house full of furniture, and I was gainfully employed with Cumberland County Schools as an adult bus driver and working at *Fayetteville Observer Times* from 9 a.m.–1 p.m. Monday through Friday. Through all the hell I was going through, I still had a goal set to reach. I wanted to have one more child by the time I turned twenty-five and, within the year after, purchase my first home.

I picked up my third job at night as adult stripper; my stage name was Carmel, which lead me to achieving my home buying goal even faster. I would travel up to New York, New Jersey, and Rhode Island, dancing and making money; it was good hard-earned money. When I was on stage, I was in my own world of happiness, and the feeling of being free from the world was everything to me; I felt *open* to life! I was dancing nude in my hometown Fayetteville, NC, at club called 37 Beautiful Girls and One Ugly Woman as well as New Jersey at the Goats. My main club was Bottoms Up on Bragg Blvd.; this is where I started initially dancing as a topless dancer. I was employed there for years prior to me branching off.

I purchased my first home at the age of twenty-six. Laverne was with me the day I went out looking for a mobile home. I found one I liked; it was beautiful! It was a must! I needed a cosigner, and she cosigned for me. The price of the mobile home was $65,000. I gave them $5,500 as a down payment on the modular home; my monthly payments were $623.00 a month. It was four bedrooms and two baths with living room, den, kitchen with an island, and dining room. They delivered the home, and I eventually had it bricked in, which costed $3,500 with a nice porch on front and deck on the back.

I had one acre of land, which I also fenced in, costing a total of $2,500. Everyone figured Thomas paid for it all. Neither Thomas, Laverne, Lucas, nor my grandmother had anything to do with my home and what it took for me to make it complete. I was called the neighborhood mom for years. All the kids would come over and hang out at "Mama Jen's house." Today they still say call me "Mama Jen" even though I had five children of my own; we still had a great time, and I always showed them the same love as I gave my own children. I would cook fish on Fridays, and they would play in the pool, and I would cook on the grill on the weekends. I started going out to Lumber Bridge, hanging out with some of my old friends from back in the day, me and a few my girlfriends.

Loc and I ended up connecting again; things became a little serious with us as years started to go by. Loc would come over and chill sometimes during the week, and on the weekends, his friends would come over and connect with some of my girls. We always had a good time that lasted for a while until Laverne would start just popping up out of nowhere. There went the enjoyment; things started to unfold rapidly. I started saying to my girlfriends, "I'm paying $623.00 a month for a double wide I can't even enjoy and land I'm paying $236.00 a month and can't walk on it in peace. *Why! Why! Why* did I give her a key again?"

It was supposed to be used only if something was needed if she happened to be watching the kids while I worked. She started using the key for her leisure, and she didn't care for Loc. He was selling narcotics at the time. Laverne didn't like anyone I dated, male or female for that matter. Loc and I were spending the weekend together. I'm bumping Styles P's "Good Times (I Get High)." I'm in my bathtub, chilling; I have my candles lit, my Calgon bubble bath going on. I'm smoking me a nice blunt of Blue Berry Hydro; the aroma in the bathroom smelled like blueberries.

Loc is at the bar rolling him a blunt of Arizona and drinking some Courvoisier on the rocks. I'm playing with the bubbles in the tub with my feet and legs. I put the blunt down and took a sip of my Tanqueray on ice when I looked up Loc was standing there in the double doors with them broad shoulders and long dreads lying on his smooth cocoa chocolate skin, smoking his blunt and holding his glass of Courvoisier on the rocks, watching me as his always did. He knew I loved to be watched; it turned me on in a way words can't describe. I immediately started to masturbate! When I finished, I got out of the tub, dried off, and lay across the bed, and Loc rubbed my body down with baby oil as he usually did. All the rubbing and massaging kicked things up. Although we were already liquored up, there is nothing like a good ole liquor dick!

The sex was heated up for a while. I was stroking him up and down; I lean forward and suck on his neck when I rise; I'm still riding like a cowgirl from Texas! Loc's eyes started to change they were moving from side to side in motion, then they were stuck in his left position but to my right position. I turned my head to the right looked around behind me and there Laverne was at my bedroom door, watching us through a one-inch crack in the door.

Loc said, "Damn, what's up, Miss Laverne, you all right?"

Laverne slowly closes the door; it was the look in her eyes that was so demonizing.

I jumped up and cut off the music. We immediately got dressed; by the time we got out there, she was gone. We saw the back of my cousin's Caprice going down Twiggs Court. Later, I had a conversation with her about being disrespectful; of course, it didn't go well at all. In Laverne's head, she felt she had a right to due to the fact she cosigned for me to get the mobile home. Our conversation did no good; she still returned. One Saturday, Loc and I were getting ready to head to Myrtle Beach for the weekend to celebrate me getting my childcare license to open my childcare center, Sweet Lullaby's Home Daycare. I was in the kitchen cooking us a good breakfast—pancakes, sausage, grits, eggs, and toast.

We just finished smoking a blunt a piece; now we were ready to eat like we were at IHOP for real. The side entrance of the mobile home is where we heard the door open to enter the dining room from the washroom of the mobile home. We turn our heads; Laverne stops in her tracks. I believe in my heart she was trying to sneak up on us with that butcher knife. She yelled at Loc, saying, "I hate you! You bastard!" As she was yelling this, she threw the butcher knife toward his face. It just barely missed his eye. We both ducked. I yelled at her, telling her to get out. "I'm calling the police. This is the last time."

She wouldn't leave; when I called Cumberland County police, she got up and left. Loc and I went to Walmart in Hope Mills and purchased locks. We changed them the same day. That didn't stop us from going on our trip. See, Laverne despised anyone she couldn't put fear in or control, and Loc stood up to her in a respectful way. Time went on, and I eventually overcame my madness of her actions toward us.

It was a dreary and still day in March. The weather outside was about 75 degrees when I peeped my head out the door as my house phone rings. It was Laverne asking for a ride to the store, which I will never understand because she had possession of my cousin's Caprice at the time. I told her I'd come take her to the store; she wanted to go to IGA in Hope Mills. After about thirty minutes of us of shopping in IGA, my cell phone rings, and it's my neighbor from across the street. He was livid; he said, "You need to get home now. The police are all over your house, and the Channel 11 news is out here too."

I told Laverne we had to go and go now!

She said, "What's wrong?"

I said, "I don't know!"

Well, when I made the right turn onto Twiggs Court off Parkton road, my heart skipped a beat. I didn't have any emotions; I was numb all over. There was a big white truck in my front yard; they were tagging everything in my house and loading it on the truck. When I turned into my yard, the police surrounded my car with guns taller than me. They had on all black; I couldn't see anything but their eyes! Our two-year-old son Yrre jumps from the backseat on top of my head; he was scared to death and screaming. The police kept yelling telling me, "Get out of the jeep now!"

I yelled back, telling them, "Put them damn guns down now or I'm not getting out. My son is scared! Back away from my damn Jeep!" I got Yrre calm down. I turned and looked at Laverne; she was sitting there trying to act so surprised about what was going on now.

23

I went in the house. I asked them, "Why are you all tagging my furniture and taking it out the house?"

They said, "Mrs. Ceasar, you have to pay taxes on the narcotics that were found in here." The officer said, "Mrs. Ceasar, you are under arrest selling narcotics to an undercover and maintaining and dwelling with controlled substance." My son Nicholas was *irate* as they took me out of the house in handcuffs. He was running beside the police, trying to get them to let me go.

The police told Nicholas if he didn't calm down, they would have to retain him.

Nicholas said, "I don't care, let my mother go!" Then he ran to the people when they were taking my belongings out the house, trying to take it back from them and put it in the house. My other children were crying and yelling. They took me to the Sheriff's Annex on 301 in Fayetteville, NC, only for me to discover Laverne was the one calling and tipping them off as he stated he showed me the paperwork with her name in it and every time she called and what was said to them. He said after a certain number of calls is when they decided to set things up! He said, "Mrs. Ceasar, listen, we know Loc was not a big drug dealer as Laverne was saying he was." He said, "But after so many calls, we have to take action."

The officer said now, "Department of Social Services are on the way to get your children."

I said, "Where are they taking my kids?"

He said, "Downtown to social services." He asked if I had any family members that could come and get them. "You would need to find a way to call and have someone pick up your children."

So I went back to asking more questions. I said, "Sir, can you tell me why I'm being charged with serving undercover?" I said, "I've never sold to an undercover before!"

His response was "Yes, you did!"

I said, "When?"

He said, "Do you recall that day a Caucasian woman came to the house with Tim?"

I said "Yeah," he said that lady was the undercover.

He said, "Mrs. Ceasar, I know you didn't have anything to do with what was going on. The day they came, you went to the normal location and nothing was there, so you called Loc. And the first thing you did was curse him out. Your words to Loc were 'I told you not to have shit else in my damn house!' Loc told you to 'give her the two doves that's all in the house!'

"You tried to give it to Tim; Tim told you, 'No, give it to her,' and you did," he said. "You then asked Loc where the rest of it at. You were taking it out the house now. Loc tells you, 'There is nothing else in the house, calm down, go look again. I moved it all out the other week when you told me!'"

So I asked the officer, "Well, where did y'all find the drugs at today?"

The officer said, "Loc didn't have any narcotics in your home initially, Mrs. Ceasar. We had Tim to call and tell Loc he wanted 3 oz. of cocaine. Loc's response was 'I don't handle that amount like that. I can contact my man and see. I'll call you back.' the officer said, "Loc called Tim back and told him to give him 30 minutes and come by." The officer said after Loc arrived at the house, they waited to make sure he was not coming back outside before they made, they move to ram the door in.

He said, "We looked and couldn't find anything but a scale. Then your toilet in the master bedroom started to overflow out of nowhere, and we ripped the toilet seat up off the floor got the 3 oz. of cocaine that he just went to get for Tim."

After the questioning, they took me to Cumberland County Detention Center, and I was under $150,000 bond. I stay in jail seven days. I remember calling some days, and Laverne wouldn't answer my phone calls at all. I was only calling to see what was going on with my kids. Being arrested was the most degrading part of my life. I'm not referring to the part when you have to bend over, spread your cheeks, and cough, take all your tracks in your head, and walk around looking like someone out of a zombie movie. It was when I came out of my cell for the first time of being locked back, and I saw myself on the news walking with my new jewelry on my wrist and hands behind my back, looking cute as always with my toffee-colored camouflage jean suite on and boots to match. This was the most degrading part of my life anyone could ever imagine.

They ran this arrest on the Channel 11 news for over a week only because I had not taken down my day care sign. I had already turned in my childcare license; I just didn't want to take down my sign. It was so beautiful, and besides, it cost too damn much. I was lucky I had the cell by myself. I couldn't eat that food; it didn't smell right, let alone look right. I just drunk the juice every day and ate crackers whenever they had some. I thought about a lot of things during those seven days in Cumberland County jail.

I had two visitors and no money on my account. On that third day, the guard brings me a pink slip. I read over the slip; it said *Denise*. The amount of money she had left was $5. I said, "This is all she had. My cousin Denise loves me." The days and nights were the longest days of my life! You can hear the guards coming as their keys jingled on their waist, the doors clicking, and the walls sliding to let us in and out. I was traumatized for years; the sound of keys would rattle my insides, make the hairs on my arms stand up, and turn my stomach upside down.

Every day the lady would get my plate and she would say, "You're not eating. You have to eat."

I said, "No, ma'am, I can't eat that food; it don't smell right." So it came to be the sixth day of me being incarcerated.

She said, "Ok, you need to eat a little of this food today, Mrs. Ceasar. If you don't, on day seven, you will be put in solitary confinement."

I said, "Are you serious right now?"

She said, "Yes, ma'am."

I knew if no one else was coming to my rescue, it would be my middle two sons' father Nelson, and sure thing he came up with $1500, and my Aunt Frances helped with a couple of hundred. It was a period in my life to be remembered of how your own family your own flesh and blood will be so *trifling* and *treacherous* and grin in your face. Nelson came, and I was released; I just knew I had to get my children, but I couldn't.

I had to wait until my whole case was over and solved. I could only see them on certain days and times. I was blessed, relieved, and thankful that my family members had them. Loc ended up getting eight years because he was a three-time felon. Our son Yrre had to live without his father for eight years of his life; he was two years old at the time. These were the most important years of his life as a child. My son had to receive counseling for years to cope with not having his father in his life.

He was petrified of the police; it didn't matter who was around or where we were at, he would have a fit. Before my children were released back to my care, I had to take AA classes weekly, drug classes weekly, parenting classes weekly, and all three were drug testing me weekly. I was on probation for one year. I was also being drug tested weekly; it was the longest six months of my life. I currently have a Class A misdemeanor on my record, which is highest charge of misdemeanor; it's next to a felony.

CHAPTER 3

It does not matter about the amount of ice in the glass; cream always floats to the top. Just as the sun sets, it will rise again.
—Jenifer Stewart

(1972–2010)

NELSON GOT THE bail money up. I was released. I asked him to take me to the house so I could check my mail. The entire ride was silent; all sorts of things were going through my mind. I was first trying to figure out how I could start picking up the pieces before I could put them together. When we made the right turn onto Twiggs Court, I checked the mail. I had received my acceptance letter for the LPN Program at Fayetteville Technical Community College. As hard as I worked to be accepted into the program, that didn't even excite me.

I was still numb from the whole ordeal; the only thing I wanted was my five husbands whose little hearts where shredded to pieces about their mother. I never viewed Laverne the same again. I told myself I would never have anything to do with her again. That was a deep cut below the belt. I just never could understand why and how someone could do their only child the way she did me, knowing her grandchildren would feel the effects from it.

I never confronted Laverne about the situation; to this day, she has no clue I knew she demolished our lives! My son Yrre suffered mentally for eight years wanting his father; his bond was broken with his father on that dreary and still March day.

Lucas heard I was accepted into the LPN Program. He said, "Well, I'll put you in one of my houses rent free." He was aware that in order to be successful in the program, it's best not to work at least not a full-time job. I was so excited to be reunited with my kids again. My six months had just passed.

I completed all the necessary obstacles the state of North Carolina had laid out for me in order to become my kids' guardian again. We moved in the house. Life was going great; Nelson was back to getting his two sons on the weekends. Yrre, Nick, and Traveon would go over to Margaret's house on the weekends. One weekend, the kids were gone, and my girlfriend Janetta was spending the weekend with me. Lucas called and said he is in town.

I say to him, "My girlfriend wants to meet you. She has heard so much about you."

He said, "I'll stop by in a few hours."

I said, "Ok." Janetta and I went to go eat at the Chinese restaurant.

We came back to my house and were talking and laughing until the doorbell rang; it was Lucas. I introduced them to one another. Janetta had on these Redskin boots with heels from out of this world! Her hips were hugging her jeans, and her breast was saying, "Hi, it's nice to meet you, Lucas." Janetta had no clue that the Redskins were his favorite team. We talked for a few minutes. He asked Janetta to step aside so he could speak to her, and when he came back in the kitchen, he said, "Janetta is going to ride with me. I'll bring her back in a few hours." They hit it off from the jump! Well, when I saw or heard anything from either one of them, it was the next morning.

I was trying to figure out what kind of inconsequential individual you are to take your daughter's lover and screw her on first sight. Lucas clearly knew she was my lover; we kissed in front of him before she left my house to ride with him. Lucas paid her well for her climax. They had sexual relations for some years on in. As they grew closer, he would pay her to take stark naked pictures and sexy photos in her lingerie outfits. What Lucas didn't know was I was the one taking all the photos of her. He wanted photos with her double-barreled shotgun between her legs, photos of her holding it in the crack of her fat ass, photos of her sucking on the barrel with her fingers in her vagina.

He would pay her $200–$300 a photo. It's demented because the same gun was the one she would put in my vagina during our sexual relations, and I never would've visualized me having to take pictures and send to my father. That was some absurd shit! I took Janetta with me to New York on my run to reup on my handbags. On the way back, I stopped by Lucas's house in Virginia. He suggested that we stay and get some sleep and leave the next morning. I told him Janetta and I could sleep in the room I always sleep in when I go to his house. Lucas said, "No! Janetta is going to sleep on the bottom level."

I said "Ok," so he tells me to show her the room she will be sleeping in.

Janetta said, "Girl, this house is nice. How many floors is it?"

I said, "It's three levels." I made sure she was comfortable and went back up to the second level floor.

The next morning, my stepmother had breakfast cooked for us before we left to head back to North Carolina. She had the table set up buffet style; Shoney's Restaurant had nothing on her. What I've always loved about her she always has some type of fruit for breakfast. We finished our fulfilling breakfast, and we thanked my stepmother for it and got our belongings and left. I stopped at the Amaco gas station outside of the neighborhood and filled up my car; when I got in the car, Janetta had this strange look on her face.

I asked her, "What's wrong?"

She said, "Nothing."

I said, "Yes, it is you looking crazy right now." I said, "Look, it's cold as fuck out here, ok, I'm trying get home and chill."

She said to me, "Don't every bring me back to your father's house again!"

I said, "What happened?"

She said, "I didn't get any sleep. All night long, he kept coming downstairs trying to sleep with me. He was rubbing all on me and begging. I kept telling him no! He was not going for that."

I said, "I know damn well you didn't sleep with him and his wife was upstairs now!"

She said, "Yes, I did. He wouldn't leave me alone."

I said, "That's some foul fucked-up ass shit there now. I won't be sucking and licking your ass for a minute, not even your ass hole!"

It was a silent a ride all the back to Carolina. Now I would have never in a billion years thought Lucas would go downstairs and have sexual encounters with my lover again in the same house his wife is in; she was on the second floor with me in the other bedroom. We made it back safe. I took Janetta home and assisted her with her belongings.

I went and picked up my football team, and we went home. Of course, they asked what their grandfather was doing. I told him, "Nothing special." I continued to attend school, making my flyers and business cards for the cleaning business I was starting. I had been asking Janetta if she wanted to be partners with me; she didn't seem to be enthused about the idea. Being persistent as I am, I kept asking her until she agreed. I named it B&J Cleaning Company! Our business was going well until Janetta start discussing with Lucas how well we were doing. Lucas started having Janetta clean his properties and not tell me what she was doing; he paid her well and told her to keep the money for herself.

Janetta's conscience was eating at her. She couldn't help but tell me. I asked her, "How could you do that? It's really not your business. You didn't want to have part in it at all! And then you going to go out and clean Lucas's properties under my name and keep the money like he told you!"

I no longer had Janetta for a business partner; instead we remained lovers. I continued to travel up to New York, getting my handbags and going to nursing school. The LPN Program was nothing to play with, besides the fact Laverne never gave me and Janetta no kind of peace. She despised her; she would call all the time, leaving unpleasant messages on her answering machine. Her behavior never ceased our relationship. At this point, I needed a mini vacation. I found a Carnival Cruise Line deal setting sail to the Bahamas for three days at the cost of $270 a piece, so I purchased it for Janetta and me.

We were all excited; it was her first time going. Prior to the trip, I had informed Laverne that I would be going out of town and I might need her to watch the kids for three days. I told her, "The ship leaves out on Thursday and returns on Sunday. She said, "Ok." This was the week of Sept 11, 2001, when World Trade Centers were bombed. I had packed my bags earlier on in the week and made plans to stay over Janetta's house the night before so we could do last minute shopping. We were out all that morning and evening, going from here to there and back to here. Before all of this, I had asked Laverne if she needed anything at all. She said, "No, if I need something, I'll go and get it." My cell phone kept ringing over and repeatedly.

I looked at it and said, "Ok, it's Laverne. I'll call her back later when I'm done."

She then begins to ring Janetta's cell phone in the same manner. The running from here to there and back to here was over; we went on to Janetta's house and finished getting our last-minute items together. Janetta checked her answering machine, and Laverne left a message cursing worse than any sailor who has ever lived. She said, "I hope that damn ship sinks while you two bitches are on it."

Janetta said, "What's wrong with your momma? Is she crazy? I should call the police on her for leaving a message like this on my answering machine."

Janetta was so scared she didn't want to go on the cruise. Laverne stayed on the prowl, a path of destruction to contaminate and poison individuals' minds along with destroying their homes and life. At times, I often wondered if she got off on demolishing peoples live as she did! Our plans continued; we had a wonderful time on our vacation. When I returned home, I had received a letter from my attorney's office informing me to contact the office immediately!

34

I called him, and he said to me, "I apologize for this matter. On the other hand, there is a warrant for your arrest."

I said, "How? I haven't missed any court dates!"

He said, "Somehow your court dates where changed, and I was not informed until now. I am advising you to lay low until I can get this taken care of in the system right now. The bounty hunters are looking for you, and they will arrest you on sight."

I said, "I have to miss school? I'm in the nursing program. I can't miss days like that. We are going through three and four chapters a week."

He said, "If you are arrested, your bond will be doubled from the original bond you had when you were arrested initially. If you are captured, your bond will be $300,000."

I instantly had flashbacks of my seven days in Cumberland County Detention Center and agreed to lay low. I immediately starting pack my bags and left Fayetteville. I called my ex-girlfriend and told her what had happened. She told me to come and stay at her place until my attorney contacted me and told me it was clear. When I was cleared, the first place I went was to FTCC to speak with my instructors.

I explained to them what happened, and they said the best thing for me was to withdraw and reapply for the program. They said we had already gone through four chapters and we had started the beginning of four more this week. Of course, I told Lucas what happened, and he said to me he was giving me and his grandchildren forty-eight hours to evacuate his house. He said, "You're lying." He said, "You didn't want to hang with it." He didn't want to hear anything else I had to say. I tried to show him proof, and he refused that as well. His sister called and picked on us when Nick would answer the phone. She was so humored at the fact he was putting us out the house in forty-eight hours.

The sad part of it all is I just reunited with my kids. I reached out to Nelson, and I told him what was going on. He asked what I needed him to do. I was letting him know that we were packing up things for right now, and in between times, we would be out riding to find another house. We found a place in Montibello on Cliffdale Road; we moved there and got settled in. I had purchased a new car. I needed Nelson's stepdad to paint it for me. The day I took my car there, Laverne was riding with me. I went there to see Carlos to find out what he would charge to paint my car and add flakes. I've been with the family for many years; what I couldn't understand was how Laverne came to be so interested in Carlos.

She started making comments about how good looking he was with his gold tooth and hair. Carlos's brothers and Nelson were there working for him. Nelson's mother, Mrs. B, and I were extremely close, closer than most people would ever imagine for an ex-mother-in-law and daughter-in-law. There was nothing I couldn't ever ask Mrs. B for; she didn't provide or assist me prior to me having her two grandsons. She was always real with me from day one. During the time I was in relationship with Nelson, we took a lot of family trips to Alabama and Florida. Our relationship was good outside of the incidents of Laverne intervening and causing chaos with Nelson about his two sons.

She always gave him hell; it was times she just straight up told him she didn't like him. I stopped by the shop on another day to bring Nelson some lunch. Mrs. B spotted me when I pulled up, and I could tell by the look on her face and that smile she had something to tell me or ask; her gold tooth was sparkling and twinkling like a star. The only thing was Laverne was sitting right here, and I didn't want her to hear anything

Mrs. B was going to say. I couldn't get out the car fast enough. Mrs. B made it to the car before I got out and asked me, "Are you going to Alabama for Carlos's father's birthday party?"

I said, "You know I'm going! When is it? When y'all leaving? How long y'all staying?"

Mrs. B said, "We going to be down there for the weekend."

Before I could say, "I'm going to book my room today," Laverne invites herself.

"I'm going, Mrs. B. Y'all don't mind, do you?"

She said, "No, come on. We're going to have a good time."

I said to myself, *Damn. Why me, Lord? I can't catch a damn break!*

I told Nelson I'd see him at the house. We left three days later for Alabama. We arrived in Alabama. Boy, did we party. It was the whole backyard, music playing inside and outside; everyone was drinking and enjoying themselves, playing cards and talking noise. Nelson and I were coming out of the house to go outside chill and mingle a little. As we were making our way through the crowd in the house, we entered the living room, and there Laverne sits with Carlos's brother-in-law who sells life insurance.

Nelson said, "What's going on over here?"

Laverne said, "I'm switching life insurance companies."

Nelson said, "Damn, Mrs. Laverne, you ain't ask me or Jenifer nothing. You just going to sign up for life insurance for our kids like that?"

The life insurance man said, "Well, I assumed you all was aware."

Nelson said, "Fuck no! What kind of shit y'all doing here?"

So once we calmed down, insurance man explained in clear and concise details to us how the policy would work.

37

Nelson and I asked the name of the insurance company, and he told us. The insurance man went on to say, "Jenifer and her children will be riders on her policy. If Jenifer passes, then Laverne gets $100,000 for her."

Nelson and I asked the same question at the same time: "If something happens to our kids, how much would Laverne receive?"

The insurance man said, "She will not receive anything. The money will go to Jenifer; they are her children. All of them are riders. The check will be made out to Jenifer in amount of $25,000."

Nelson and I both asked, "Are you sure?"

He said, "Yes."

I signed all the necessary paperwork there was to sign in reference to the policy. We went on outside to finish enjoying the party. It was a muggy Alabama night with enjoyment in the air. I started dancing. I was wearing my long black dress, the one I called the Tony Braxton dress; it was black with sliver stones engraved in it with slits on both sides that reached my cheeks. The back was cut low, down to the top of my bottom. The front was cut with an oval shape, and the strings wrapped around my neck. I had on my sliver shoes; the straps laced up to my thighs. I was turning heads that night. The more I danced, the more Nelson poured his Courvoisier in his glass with no rocks; the attention was killing him. As the night dwindled down, we ate some good ole down-home Southern food before we returned to the room.

The party was over, and we returned to our room only for me to see Carlos leaving the hotel. I said to myself, *What is he doing leaving from here?* Laverne had her room at the same hotel also. The Courvoisier had Nelson out; he didn't witness what I did. I knew for a fact Mr. B's room was on the other end of the main road. In my mind, I started wondering and thinking back to Laverne's past actions. I said, "It can't be so! We all the way down here. I know she ain't trying to be stealthy and getting it on with Carlos." Sunday came, and we left to come back to North Carolina. I dropped Laverne off first. When she got out of the car, I told Nelson that I thought I had seen Carlos coming from the hotel we stayed at.

His response was "It's his hometown. He could've been coming from meeting one of his friends."

I said to myself, *I don't think so.*

The following weekend, I was turning into Laverne's apartments and saw Carlos backing out from the parking spot directly in front of her apartments. I said I knew it was so. The first chance I got, I called Mrs. B and told her.

She said, "Ummm, huh, I got you, and I'm going to take care of it."

Mrs. B put fire in Carlos's ass! She brought that fling to an end. I went to Laverne's house that Sunday; she was infuriated as hell.

She said, "You wait until Monday! I'm calling IRS on Carlos's ass! I am going to fix him."

I asked her, "What are you talking about? Why are you so mad?" I said, "Don't call the IRS. You are going mess everybody up!"

She called and said Carlos and Mrs. B were passing out W-2 forms like hot cakes; Laverne was very much aware who all received them.

The IRS audited them for documentation of proof. Their accountant had died; his office was at a house. Someone else took over at the house, and it had burned down. Well, they

39

couldn't provide IRS with the original documentation they were requesting. Nelson and I were caught up in the audit. Everyone had to pay taxes back for the years they were audited.

We filed each year, and they kept our entire tax check. I didn't receive taxes for three years, and Nelson didn't receive his taxes for five years. This was hard on Nelson and me. We were living together and weren't receiving taxes for some years. The day I purchased my first car, it was Honda Accord in a champagne color and with a sunroof. Laverne was with me. As I was pulling off the car lot to come back to Fayetteville, she looked at me and said, "I envy you now that you have this car. Now take me home!"

I dropped her off at her apartment in Clinton, and I was on my way to Fayetteville to show Nelson my car. When I got there, I asked Nelson, "What does envy mean?"

He said, "Someone is jealous of you and don't like you."

I said, "Laverne said that to me."

He said, "What is wrong with her?"

I said, "I figured that's what that meant. I just wanted to hear it from you."

I would never understand how one woman can be so spiteful, devious, hateful, mean, and deadly! Laverne is always quoting Bible scriptures and posting them on social media; behind closed doors, she is Satan in the flesh and evil. She can get anyone to believe anything she says. She is good for saying she thinks twenty-four hours a day. She is known for telling someone she will tie their tongues.

CHAPTER 4

It does not matter about the amount of ice in the glass; cream always floats to the top. Just as the sun sets it, will rise again.
—*Jenifer Stewart*

(2011–2021)

I STARTED A new job at KGP Logistics in Hope Mills, NC, on Technology Dr. in the year 2011, a month after I received my bachelor's in health administration. This is where I met my second husband; his name is Nickolas. Nickolas and I would talk after work for hours during our first thirty days of knowing one another. I zipped through my entire life within those thirty days. Things continued to progress with Nick and me for months and months, which turned into years.

We experienced a couple of tragedies within the first few months. We lost our first child in the month of October 2011 after we had seen the heartbeat for the first time. I woke up in the middle of the night in the worst pain I had ever felt in my life. I went to the doctor; first thing that morning, the doctor did an ultrasound and showed me where the sac had started to detach from the womb. My world was crushed. I said to God, "This was an experience you wanted me to have. I've been pregnant thirteen times and had six boys and I've never experienced a miscarriage until now."

I was out of work for short time. I returned to work only to hear they might be relocating to Atlanta the following year. Nick moved in; we were living our best life, taking trips to Atlanta. I was selling handbags; he would ride with me to reup on my handbags. I would be in there doing my usual inspecting the handbags I wanted to purchase. "Quality is #1 to me."

Nick looked at me and said, "Wow! You are really a hustler! You know how to hustle."

I said to Nick, "I've been hustling for years in so many ways." I said, "This is my favorite out of all."

He asked, "Why?"

I said, "Because I get to travel and see the world meet different people, and it's always a different experience on every *run I make!*"

Nick asks, "How long have you been selling handbags?"

I said, "Over fifteen years." I said, "My homeboy Playboy from back in the day turned me on to this hustle. You probably have seen him before; he would be on Murchison Rd. across from Tony's store in the parking lot of the grandmother's washerette, selling his bags. When I was dancing, I would always go to him and grab me a duffel bag or handbag. Playboy would always say, 'Come on, Jenny, you need to get on this. You could make some good money selling these pocketbooks, girl!'

"So one day I took Playboy up on his offer, and he took me on road trips up top to New York and showed me the ropes. I took off from there. I was making trips only on the weekends and once a week, then those trips turned into to me going on runs two to three times a week for a while. As my sales grew, my trips started to shorten. I was able to buy bigger quantities. I've taken many trips alone, and sometimes my homegirls might roll, but if I can't find someone to ride, that didn't stop me. I'm going to get it regardless."

Nickolas asked, "Well, why are you coming to Atlanta now?"

I said, "My man I've been dealing with for years up top has a spot in Atlanta also. We are pulling into the parking lot; this is it right here where we are now." I said, "The last couple of runs I've made alone coming here. The police are getting to be bad now. They just raided the flea market in Raleigh and confiscated millions of dollars in merchandise.

"The flea market on Bragg Blvd. just got raided too. I hate to stop selling my handbags, but I refuse to have a replay of seven years ago. It was when I took my last trip to ATL alone; all along I-20, the police were starting to just randomly pull cars over and sitting their merchandise on the side of the road and calling for backup; they had vans and trucks loading up people's merchandise. I would pray to God to allow me to get to my destination safely and back. I'm only trying to feed my kids; the money was good. It good, just like my home boy Playboy told me; my clientele was humongous!"

Nick and I had a good conversation going and coming from Atlanta that weekend. We clocked in at 10:30 as scheduled Monday morning. As I'm case shipping AT&T products, my supervisor came to get me and told me it's an emergency and I need to leave work. He received a call from Laverne stating she was sick and needed to be taken to hospital. I clocked out to go to her apartment. On Legion Road, she changed her mind and said she was not going anywhere; she felt ok.

I ask her, "How did you get well so fast? I worked right there on off 301, not ten minutes away!" I asked her, "Are you putting on?" I said, "Ma, I can't be messing up my money!"

The weekend came; Nickolas and I went on a trip to Virginia Beach. There, we were relaxing; my cell phone rang—Laverne on another stunt as the other week, claiming to be sick. She needed go to hospital, and she was about to pass out.

I said, "You're going to have to call 911. I'm not in town." Her whole tone changed in her voice. She had the nerve to say, "You and that man are always going somewhere, my God!"

I believe it was this weekend I conceived our second child.

I had another miscarriage two months later. I was out of work for another short time. When I returned to work three months later, KGP Logistics moved to Atlanta, GA. Nick asked me if I was going to relocate to Atlanta.

I said, "No, they not offering more money and not paying us to relocate." I asked him "Are you going?"

He said, "No."

Nick came over when we got off work. I happened to be on the computer looking up jobs in Florida. He asked what I was doing.

I said, "Doing some research I've been doing for some time now."

His response was "Oh, you moving to Florida?"

I said, "Just as fast as I can!"

He had a puzzled look on his face.

In March 2012, KGP Logistics relocated, and a month later, we relocated to Sanford, FL. I went to works as a teacher doing sign language with special needs children who were autistic. Nick was working at the airport in Sanford, FL. Life was beyond great in this sunshine state. It was so great; God answered my prayers for me to give Nick a child. After year in Florida, we moved back to North Carolina. Almost five months later, I found out I was pregnant for the third time with our son Tylilrius. Everyone always complimented his name; he was named after his five brothers. He passed away at six months from medical malpractice reasons in Chapel Hill.

This was life changing experience to lose my seventh son six days after my birthday on October 17, 2017. Nick asked me to marry him the next morning after Tylilrius passed. Laverne was at our house, and as I walked down the hall, I called her name. I said, "Laverne, guess what Nick asked me?"

She said, "What?"

I said, "He asked me to marry him."

She said, "Oh, really!"

We had guests coming in to sit with us in a few hours. I went in the garage to get more chairs so everyone would be comfortable. While I was in the garage, my cell phone rang. It's Lucas. I was also having moment crying like a baby; my son hadn't been dead a complete twenty-four hours.

I said, "Hello."

Lucas said to me, "Jenifer. he is better off dead. If he would've lived, he would've been a sick little boy anyway." Somehow Lucas got wind of Nick asking me to marry him in the same conversation. Lucas said, "Don't marry him."

I said, "I am going to marry him."

He said, "I'll pay you $2,000 a month not to marry him, buy you an SUV! And put you in one of my houses. Just don't marry him."

I was so blowed from what I was hearing that I couldn't comprehend anything. The conversation ended, and I went back in the house. The doorbell rang; it was my mother-in-law, father-in-law, and their first cousins. The people were starting to come in and sit a while.

I was sitting in the living room talking to my in-laws about Tylilrius, and Laverne called my name for the second time, asking me the same questions. She said, "I need to know when are y'all going to have the memorial service?"

I said, "Kevin said there is no rush because he is being cremated." I said, "He just died yesterday why do you keep asking? It's no rush, and I have company out here right now."

She said, "Well, my pastor wants to do the service."

I said, "Ok, but I'm not sure when it will be."

I walked back to the living room and sat down. Then the doorbell rings again; it was my best friend, Shakeia. We went to sit down in the kitchen. As we are talking, Laverne called my name again. I just shook my head.

I went to see what she wanted again. This time she had her pastor on the phone, and she said, "My pastor is on the phone, and he wants to know when the memorial service is going to be."

I said, "Ma, I just told you three times already today. I don't know. My mental state ain't good. I'm not up for anything. He just died yesterday. Why do you keep asking me same thing? I said don't worry about it. Nick has two home churches he attends. One of their pastors can do the memorial service."

She said, "You're not going to inconvenience my pastor; he has things he has to do."

I said, "Let him do what he has to do. Forget it." I walked back to the kitchen where Shakeia was and told her, "Come on, let's go in the garage and sit in the car."

I was telling Shakeia my uncle's funeral was that weekend and I had to go. I didn't want to miss his funeral.

The next thing I know, the garage door opened. Laverne yelled, "You are an ungrateful bitch! And that's not your uncle, that's my uncle. You didn't have a relationship with him, I did!" She looked at Shakeia and said, "I hate you, you black bitch!" She then said, "Y'all kiss my big fat black ass!" She slammed the door.

She started raising so much hell my in laws got up and was going to leave and Nick told his parents and first cousins, "Sit back down, everything is ok!" I was so embarrassed and hurt; I hadn't been able to grieve or process how I was going to do my son's memorial or when I wanted to have the memorial service.

This was what I had to deal with not even twenty-four hours later from Laverne in my own home. I was ready for her deranged ass to get the fuck out of my house pronto! She just continued to snap out in front of guess as they came for no reason; people would just get up and leave. Prior to Shakeia leaving, she looked at me and said, "I'm sorry you have to deal with this. You've been going through this for too long." Shakeia was shattered by her experience with Laverne's actions toward me and her; even though it was not her first one, it was the situation at hand that had her so fraught.

I was so sick of being embarrassed by Laverne's deranged actions all the time. On the third day, Laverne started inquiring about the death certificate—when was it coming—she needed it so she could contact insurance company. This became a song she was just singing.

I said, "Nick, she knows damn well that death certificate is not going to be ready in three days. Why does she keep asking me?" I took it upon myself to call the insurance company. I explained to them my mother was inquiring about the death certificate, so I wanted to know if she would explain to me how the disbursement of the funds would go.

The insurance lady did her verification process, and she went on to say, "All monies will come to you. It's your child; you all are just riders on her policy."

So I said to the insurance lady, "I feel like I'm going to have problems with Laverne when this is clear."

The insurance lady said, "It's good that you called to ask questions."

I said, "I know how my mom can be when it comes to certain things."

The insurance lady then asked me for the address to verify she had the right one for me. She read the address, and I said no that is an old address. So I asked her, "Should I go head and tell her I called?"

The insurance lady said, "You can, or you don't have to. It's your money, Mrs. Ceasar."

I said, "Well, I know I'm going to hear her mouth anyway."

She said, "Mrs. Ceasar, I know this is a difficult time for you, but to be honest, I've been doing this for years, and if your mother is entitled to anything, you can give her all the money she has paid on the policy for six months for Tylilrius while he was alive. Other than that, she is not entitled to it." The insurance lady repeated again, "If something happens to you, she gets $100,000, and your children have $25,000, and that will go to you. She don't receive any of that. you all are riders on the policy."

I informed Laverne that I called, and all hell broke loose. Laverne started calling us every day repeatedly asking, "Has the insurance check come yet?"

The kids said, "No, Grama!"

Laverne starts to get paranoid and said to her grandkids, "That damn check came. Y'all motherfuckers don't want to tell me! It's my damn money, not your mothers!"

My kids started asking me, "What's wrong with Grama, Ma?" My kids started asking me, "Ma, whose check is it? Yours or hers?" I said, "Who had Tylilrius?" I said "If it was not my check, it wouldn't be coming to this address!"

Laverne calls again, furious as hell, saying, "Just keep the damn check!"

I said, "It's my money. I'll give you the money for six months you paid on the policy for Tylilrius like the lady said I can do. You're the one that kept asking over and over for Tylilrius's social security number to add him on the policy!"

In Laverne's mind, it was still her check, and she started to say, "Well, I'll give you half of the money." She then goes on to say, "$8,000. I have to pay off all my credit cards."

Nick suggests going to Laverne's house and call the insurance company and let them tell her. We go to Clinton, and she calls the insurance company. It was a man who answered the phone this time. He told her the same the same thing the insurance man in Alabama told her. He said, "Ms. Downing, the check is not yours; your daughter and her children are riders on your policy; whatever happens to them, the money goes to her, $25,107.53 for each child.

Laverne said, "I want the check stopped now."

He said, "Ma'am, that is not possible. The policy is paid and up-to-date, and her son is deceased. She called and informed us, and the check will be going to her at her address."

She then said, "I don't remember anyone telling me that when I added my other grandchildren on the insurance policy."

The insurance man said, "Ma'am, we have paperwork right here. You have to sign saying that you agreed and you are aware of the terms and conditions."

She's still flipping out on the phone. She tells him, "I want to undo this now. What do I have to do?"

He told her he would have to fax paperwork for Jenifer Ceasar to sign, and it needed to be faxed back to us. On the other hand, the check will still go to Mrs. Ceasar.

Laverne agreed. The check came two weeks later on a Saturday. She called, asking if it came, and the kids told her I was out looking for some where to cash it. Laverne blew our cells phones up on that feel-good Carolina Saturday! She wouldn't stop calling, saying, "Don't cash my damn check. That's my money!" So we just went to Clinton.

I said, "The hell with it let's go get her. I'm sick as hell of her all way around."

We went to the check cashing place inside the BP gas station. Laverne was in the front seat. Nick was driving, and my son was in the back seat, sitting behind his grandmother. I came out the store with the money. She goes off big time; I gave her the money she had paid into the policy for the six months. She started hitting the dashboard, and she even gave Nick a lick or two saying, "Tell her to give me my damn money now before I tear this damn car apart!"

My son said, "Grama, chill out. Now you know that is not your money. Momma already called and talked to the insurance company."

My son said, "It's my brother's money. Why should she give you the whole $25,107.53 that you are not entitled to?"

Laverne did flip out then.

I said, "Take all the fucking money. I'm not going to argue over no money or be stressed. My son's life don't have a price on it; he's worth more than that."

She counted out $500 and gave it to Nick and counted out $8,000 to give to me.

My son just shook his head said, "Grama, you know you wrong for that."

We dropped her off and went to back to Fayetteville. I stopped by Margaret's house and told her what happened. She was so upset with me.

She said, "Why did you give her that baby's money? It wasn't her money; the insurance company told you that."

I told my grandmother, "I was sick and tired of fussing, yelling, and harassing."

Then we went back on Monday to take her to PNC Bank, where she put the money in CDs; she said she couldn't touch the money for seven years.

Laverne called her brother in Hope Mills and told him all kind of things. I called him, trying to talk to him; he let me have it. Laverne had told him lies as she usually does. She had promised him money; I know because she let that part slip out.

I took my kids on a trip. I've always told them I would take them to Times Square to see the ball drop we always watched it together on TV. I wanted them to have the experience. In December 2013, we had a great time in New York City. My husband and my kids had the time of their lives shopping and sightseeing.

My oldest son couldn't go; he had just become manager at the jewelry store in Cross Creek Mall, and my other oldest didn't want to go. Instead, he stayed home. I begged him to go. He didn't want to; instead, he stayed home and chased ass. When we returned; he had a girl in the house with purple hair. Nick and I came to the conclusion that we had been through a lot losing Tylilrius; he was the second son and brother the family had lost in my circle. Nick and I moved in 2014 to Orlando, FL, in March. We were living well and enjoying life and were glad to be so far away with a peace of mind. We would come home a few times throughout the year.

As September approached, Nick was trying to decide what to do for his mother's birthday. I said, "Call her and ask her what her plans are."

Nick called his mom. She said she had no plans, and he told her to come to Orlando for four days for her special day! Laverne had been calling about coming to Florida; she asked me to come get her, and I told her I had not planned on coming back that way. Nick and I were getting ready for his parents to come down for his mother's birthday.

Laverne asked, "Well, who all is coming?"

Nick said, "My mom, my dad, and my sister and her husband."

Laverne accompanied her best friend to Daytona Beach; they went to meet some guys that sing in a band. The weekend was up, and her best friend headed back. Laverne didn't ride back with her best friend. She tells her she is going on to Orlando from there and that I was coming to pick her up from the hotel. I had no recollection of that; I'm still preparing for my in-laws to come. Nick's family arrives a couple days later; it was a beautiful, bright, and sunny September day in Orlando when his family arrived. Nick and I took them sightseeing and shopping on the first day. We later returned to our house.

Laverne asked them how they liked Orlando. They told her they loved it and that they really liked Sanford, FL, which is twenty-five minutes away from Orlando, FL.

We all said that we decided to have a cookout at the park in Sanford for my mother-in-law's birthday tomorrow.

They loved the yachts, basketball courts, and tennis courts. Out there you can feed the alligators, and geese.

Laverne said, "It's going to be too hot out there!" She asked, "What time are y'all going?"

They responded, "About two o'clock or one maybe."

My mother-in-law arrived the next day; we woke up to another sunny and bright day in Orlando with blessed intentions to do make sure she enjoyed her first vacation and birthday in Florida. By one o'clock, it was 85 degrees. The wind was blowing as always, so they came to our house to follow us to the park and start the celebration for my mother-in-law.

We arrived safely. We all were setting up decorations; the backyard music was playing, and our old neighbors were out there assisting us. Next thing we knew, Laverne started blowing up our cell phones.

I answered my phone. I said, "Hello."

She said, "Come take me home. I want to go home now!"

I said, "Ma, I can't come now. We just got to the park now. I have to hang up now and go and get this stuff set up."

She steadily called and called. Nick and I ignored the calls. We figured she was going start something; it never failed. Then she started calling Nick's mother and father's cell phone.

I said, "Nick, I don't have time for her right now. She knows what we are doing."

My best friend Zakar had moved in with us.

She called Zakar's cell phone. Zakar said, "Jenifer, your

mother says she's getting ready to tear up y'all's house if don't nobody come and take her back to NC now!" Zakar laughed to no end at what Laverne kept calling and saying. Zakar said, "Boomie, what's wrong with your mama?"

I said to Nick and Zakar, "It's not going to be good when we get back."

They said they would be worried about her. I said to them, "Y'all better be. She is in a rage."

She started back calling everybody's cell phones. After a while, they started asking, "Is everything ok? She sounds pretty upset! She said she wants to go home now!"

Nicks family asked, "What happened from the time we left Orlando?"

Nick and I said nothing! I said, "That's how jealous she is that we're here with y'all."

They said, "She could've come."

I said, "No, she don't do heat. Then she would've been saying she about to pass out, and then we would have to take her back and get caught in traffic on I-4! That's not fair. It's my mother-in-law birthday and her first trip to Orlando!" I said, "Let's finish having a good time, just don't answer no more. She's just going to keep calling and cursing on the phone."

The cookout was over; we headed back to Orlando. Nick, Zakar, and I took my in-laws to their hotel on International Drive. I suggested we go out to Parliament House to give her time to cool off.

On the way from the Parliament House on that cool Orlando night, the phone starts to ring at 2 a.m. consistently. It was like she was tag teaming us the way she rang everyone's phone back to back.

I said, "Oh Lord, she's still in a rage for what!" I hated to go back home. I said, "Nick, when we get there you go in first." I suggested, "Let's go in the front door."

Nick and Zakar asked, "Why?"

I said, "We don't need to go through the garage and up the stairs, and we don't know or can't see what's coming down on us as we are going up into the house."

Nick said, "I'm not worried about nothing. She not going do anything"

I said to Nick, "You don't know my mama. She walks with the clothes basket all the time don't let the clothes basket fool you, she really don't need it. She just got dependent on it."

We entered the house, Nick first.

Boom, there it was. Laverne started raising hell, calling all of us bitches! As she was walking toward of us, she stopped at the foyer. There lay my open Bible on the twenty-third Psalm. She started banging the butcher knife on the Bible, the pages were splitting with every bang, and yelling, "All three of y'all are screwing around together! I hate y'all! Y'all left me here all day!" The more she yelled, she banged the Bible. My kids were in their rooms, walking in circles calling her name. She stopped beating the Bible with the knife. She walked toward Nick face with the same knife. She said, "I'll will cut you. If you value your life, you don't need to sleep in the house tonight, if you want to see the next day."

I told, "Nick, come on ignore her."

Zakar went and sat on the couch in living the room. Nick and I went in our room to the bathroom, then we hear her starting with Zakar.

Laverne said, "I hate you, bitch!" I came out the room to tell Laverne leave her alone.

She yelled, "No, I'm not!"

I said again, "Leave her alone." I told Zakar, "Ignore her, don't say nothing to her."

Laverne then walks closer to Zakar, yelling, "You're sleeping with them, you bitch!"

Zakar never said a word; she just sat there.

I told Laverne to leave her alone. "She is not bothering you!

Laverne said, "No! Bitch! If you valued your life, you won't go to sleep in here tonight."

I said, "You're not going to keep calling me and my friend a bitch!"

Laverne gets closer to Zakar. I told Zakar to move. "She is getting too close to you!"

Laverne said, "I'm going to bust your head open, bitch!" She took her pocket book out the clothes basket and hit Zakar in her forehead.

I said, "I'm calling Orlando police department."

Laverne said, "I don't care, call them!"

Zakar had a knot on her forehead for three days. The police arrived; it was five officers at one time. When they arrived, Laverne still had the butcher knife in her hand. The five officers said, "Ma'am, put he the knife down, please!" She didn't. They said again, "Ma'am, put the knife down!"

She threw the knife toward them but at the floor.

They said, "Ok, ma'am, we're going to have to take you to jail."

I said, "Thank you. Please get her out of here. It's 2:30 a.m."

One hour and thirty minutes later, the police department called me and said they had a difficult time trying to arrest her due to her corpulence. I said, "Ok." They had taken her to police station and gave her paperwork stating she was never to return to the state of Florida again in life!

The Orlando police department called me again about 4 a.m. asking if is there anyone's house she can go to in Orlando? I said, "No, sir, her best friend left two days ago going back to North Carolina." I told the officer, "I don't know where she can go."

My husband, being the gentleman that he is, called his sister and asked if Laverne could sleep in their room with them until they leave. She said, "Yes!"

The Orlando police took her there. Nick then spoke to his parents the next morning and he told them a little about what happened. They then decided to cut their vacation short to go back to North Carolina. Laverne rode back to North Carolina in the car with Nick's sister and her husband. It was sad they didn't come to see us before they left.

Nick's mother was always sweet and nice to Laverne before and after the fact of her actions. About two years later, we were located back in Carolina. I was back to my unnecessary usual routine, which Laverne says no one does at all, and that's traveling up and down Highway 24, going to the store for her or transporting her to Fayetteville to be ill-mannered to her own family and their friends.

One day, Laverne needed to go Walmart; on our way to Fayetteville, we stop at the Walmart in Clinton. Nick's mother worked there for many years. Well, Laverne finished shopping. Nick and I went to return the riding cart and speak to his mother before we leave. We were in the store for thirty minutes.

The weather outside was ok; it was not cold or hot. It was one of those just right days in Clinton. Nick's mother came out with us to the car, and she spoke to Laverne; she cursed his mother out so bad.

She said, "Don't speak to me, bitch. You held them up in that store for over an hour knowing I'm out her in this damn car!"

As she was saying that, Nick had a look on his face I've never seen before, an out-of-this-world look.

Nick's mother said, "I'm sorry. You go head and get on to Fayetteville"

I said, "Ma, why did you curse her out like that?"

She said, "I've been in this car over and hour. I'm ready to go. I got my grandkids' chicken salad in here!"

I said "Ma! You have not been in this car no hour. It's been thirty minutes, and it's not cold or hot out here. There was no call for the way you cursed her out. You are wrong for that."

Nick was driving; he never said a word. When we arrived at our house, he still got her bags and walker out the car and helped her in the house as he always does! Laverne never apologized for cursing out his mother; she was always quoting Bible scriptures, claiming she was a woman of God and holier than thou. She was so involved in the church to the point she was having sexual encounters with the pastor; his wife was not fond of Laverne. The first lady was very much aware of what's going on. Laverne was always bragging on how she was buying the pastor bow tie sets, cuff links, and suits. She said the wife says he won't wear the suits she buys, so Laverne takes it upon herself to start doing wifely duties. One Sunday, Laverne stated he was staring at her so hard, he called her name during the sermon he was preaching.

She started out with the mailman; that fling went on for about two years until he went back to his wife. She claims the pastor didn't care for the mailman to be at her house. She bragged all the time how the deacons in the church were always hugging on her and telling her she smelled so good.

I asked her, "Ma, why do you flirt with them deacons like that in their wives' faces?"

She said, "Ain't studding them women."

My husband told me when I had our son, she was trying to convince him that our son was his father's child! Nick says he doesn't understand why she is always talking about me to him. She has told him on several occasions she would give his father a run for his money, and then she says, "I wouldn't do your mother like that."

Through it all, we are still standing strong!

CHAPTER 5

It does not matter about the amount of ice in the glass; cream always floats to the top. Just as the sun sets, it will rise again.
—Jenifer Stewart

I'M OFTEN TOLD about how strong I am as a person. I've never been able to really see it because of everything I've allowed my cohabitants to take me through. As an individual, I've always felt like I was weak because I always go back and continue to allow them to treat me like the most hated and unwanted child that I am. You see, as child, you tend to give your parents passes to mentally and emotional abuse you. No human of any kind should have the experience of not being wanted by their parents. As the adult I am today, I recall my childhood and teenage years very well.

The emotional abuse started from me being isolated and confined to my room. I remember I couldn't go anywhere. I would beg and beg to go places with my friends or family. I remember times my aunts would say, "Let her go outside with the other kids and play." I used to sit and look out the window at the other children having fun. I literally couldn't engage in normal activities with my friends without being called a slut, whore, and bitch. It was not because I had done something and I was on punishment; those are just the destructive actions that were taken out on me by my mother. I used to have to stay in my room when I got out of school until the next school day. When she was at work, Bean would allow me to be the little girl I needed to be.

At the same time, I was being isolated, rejected, and terrorized. I'm also being rejected by my father. I would call him many of days, crying out for his help. Most of the time, he would refuse me; he would always blame it on my mother. My father had all kinds of excuses for emotionally abandoning me. He rejected me physically ever way he could; if I didn't march to the beat of his drum, he would belittle me to no end. I remember the times he would tell me, "You're not going to amount to anything. You're going to be just like your mother."

He never gave me the love and attention I was longing, begging, and crying for. With me being the only child, it's sad to know the amount of shunning I went through. The terrorizing never really ended for me in my childhood, teenage, and adult years. It just got worse over time. I've been ridiculed and humiliated my entire life. For a mother to curse, yell, and scream at me in front of my friends, coworkers, or just complete strangers in a place of business is beyond unreasonable extreme action toward the only child you have in this world. That feeling and experience are nothing like a person could ever dream of. As I matured into a young woman and adult, my mother would threaten my life at a plunge of footstep and the blink of an eye. Her actions toward me have been unacceptable. She would always try to intimidate me. I didn't want to accept the fact that my mother hated me.

She has told me and texted me for the last time. I used to feel as though losing a child was the worst pain in the world. Since I've been writing this book, I've shed a lot of tears along with having anxiety attacks. If someone were to ask me what the hardest part of my life has been, I would say having to relive my life in order to write this book. It's very painful for me. In most cases, a child has at least one parent they have a bond with or they can at least go to; in my case, I don't have either parent. It's sad when you try to go to one parent and that parent is just a bad as the first parent the only parent. I had to call was God, and I know this is how I made it through. My parents being the way they have been toward me made me the strong individual everyone says I am today! My skin is like elephant's skin.

CHAPTER 6

It does not matter about the amount of ice in the glass; cream
always floats to the top. Just as the sun sets, it will rise again.
—Jenifer Stewart

(1996, 1998, 2005, 2021)

THERE WHERE SO many times I would inform Laverne of
things, and she would always steer me away from whatever she
knew I really wanted to do. I've always wanted to drive eigh-
teen-wheelers. I love to travel and see new things. I only have
one life to live. For me, I need to see everything there is. If I
would've continued my journey of completing the necessary
steps to be successful in that area, I more than likely would've
covered majority of the United States by now. I mentioned it
to Laverne, and she told me no, that wasn't a good idea. My
kids need me.

I had already spoken to Margaret about it, and she was
willing to watch over Nick and Traveon, who were four and
six years old at the time, until I had completed truck driving
school. My plan was to drive local for a while; as they got older,
I would travel coast to coast. The truck driving class was not

that long. The school I was going to attend was in Greensboro, NC, at the time. My grandmother Margaret has always instilled in me and told me, "You only have one life to live. See as much as the world as you can while you can." My grandmother is my angel and has always been on my team regardless.

I allowed Laverne to talk me out of it; she tried to talk me out of driving the school bus by telling me, "You can't handle all the kids on a school bus. That is too much responsibility."

I said, "I'm driving the bus. It's what I want to do. You talked me out of truck driving school; you're not talking me out of this!"

I figured if I can't drive an eighteen-wheeler, then I'll go to school and get my CDLs to drive for Cumberland County school systems. The school bus was the next biggest thing for me to drive next to eighteen-wheeler. I completed Cumberland county schools bus driver's class and driver's course and received my CDLs. I worked for Cumberland County Schools for seven years as an adult bus driver. I remember the first day of work. I arrived at my bus, number 246. I stopped and look and said, "Dang, I wanted a Playskool bus with the tinted windows and AC."

When I pulled the doors open on the bus, I walked up the steps sat down and said, "OMG! It's a stick shift." I love driving stick shift cars. I wanted an automatic bus, and then I told myself, *I got this. I'm going to drive this big bitch like I drive a stick shift car.*" I was whipping Bus 246 all over the road; it was a breeze. When I pulled on Douglas Byrd parking lot to drop the kids off on my first day, the assistant principals and principal said "Girl, you whipping it, ain't you?"

I said, "It ain't too much of nothing I can't handle."

They laughed.

I loved my students; we had a bond like no other. They would sit behind me and talk to me about anything. They used to tell me I was the coolest bus driver they ever had. I would give them pizza parties two times a month. One of my students and I grew a different type of bond; it was a bond from out of this world; today Shakeia and I are like sisters/best friends. We have traveled many places together from Pensacola, FL, to New York City shopping, flirting, and enjoying one another. We are and will always be inseparable. I had my students spoiled. I would pick them up in front of the house if I didn't see them prior to me stopping. I already knew they would be running late trying to catch the bus.

During holiday time, my students would give me gifts. They brought me gifts on my birthday. I would give them gifts as well. I received the bus driver of the year award for three years in a row. After my first six months of driving, I pulled in the parking lot. Bus 246 wasn't there. I was in a panic. I said, "Where is my bus at?" I called the assistant principal. I said, "My Bus 246 is gone, and I have to get my kids. What do I do?"

They had me on speaker phone. They said, "Congratulations on your new bus, 113."

I was happy and sad!

I finally got the new Playskool-looking bus with tinted windows and AC with cameras, which I didn't care for. I was sad because I had got attached to Bus 246. It was old and raggedy, but she got down the road once I put her in second gear! In between the hours of my schedule to drive, I would go to my second job at *Fayetteville Observer Times* from 9–1 p.m. During my customer service representative years, I made top sales representative for two months in a row. Everyone gave me the *irate* customers to handle; I loved it. I remember being on the phone with this customer for three hours. At the end of the call, I had retained her. At end of the day, it's about listening to the customer and delivering top-quality service to the customer.

In the later years, I opened my day care center Sweet Lullaby's Home Daycare. This was a challenging task, getting everything to pass in order to open for business—the buildings inspections, fire department inspections, health department inspections, and North Carolina childcare state inspections. I created and designed my own flyers, business cards, and donations letters. I promoted and marketed my business in every way you could think of. Sweet Lullaby's Home Day Care Center finally received three children. They were before school children. They would arrive at 5 a.m. in the morning; their bus would come at 7:15 a.m. I continued to market to fill my open slots. I stayed open a complete year. After I was still unable to fill the slots, I then turned in my North Carolina childcare license to the state. I called my childcare consultant, and she came out and picked them up.

She said, "Mrs. Ceasar, I have to tell you again that is one nice sign you have in the yard."

I said, "Thank you!"

She asked, "Are you going to take it down?"

I said, "No, ma'am, I paid too much money for it, and plus, I might open back up again."

My son Traveon would hound me about taking it down; I would tell him no, I might reopen one day. That day never came. Laverne just knew she had me hook, line, and sinker when she set Loc up with police. What she didn't know was I had closed to business and turned in my license a very long time ago. Laverne did everything in her power through the years to destroy me.

It was unexplainable to tell anyone how it felt to have your mother to tell you she hated you. The few individuals I told asked me how it made me feel. I lied and said it didn't bother me. The only truth I told in reference to the fact was I laughed when the text came through to my cell phone and she said, "I hate you and don't you ever forget it." Now if someone was to tell me she had some sort of mental issues, then it wouldn't hurt as bad as it does. On the other hand, for me to believe she has some mental disabilities is hard for me due to the fact she was a nurse for many years, and even during those years, she told me she envied me!

That lets me know there is nothing wrong with her mental state. My father told me three years ago I was a mistake. I should've never been born. Now do I love my mother and father? Yes! I do, more than they realize! See, you have to love where you come from at the end of the day. You wouldn't be reading the book if it wasn't for them. God has the last say so! I still turned out to be *an eclectic, strong, amazing, gorgeous, exotic, stunning, and beautiful woman.*

EPILOGUE

There were some good family ties I've shared with Laverne and Lucas on separate occasions. Laverne and my favorite sport together was tennis. We would go play tennis at Rowan Street Park on the weekends. Bowling was another family sport that included her longtime boyfriend Bean and my cousins. We would take trips to Myrtle Beach, the Washington D.C. Zoo, and Asheboro Zoo. Lucas showed me how to drive a stick shift, which was his 280ZX Turbo, at twelve years old. My trips and summer vacations with Lucas were learning and inviting visits.

I would spend some holidays with him; I enjoyed all the precious moments with my brother. Lucas always said, "Those two are double trouble when they get together." Lucas would take us to the Washington Monument, the capitol, and the Thomas Jefferson Memorial. I couldn't come home until I went back to the Washington Monument. I called it "the pencil." He took us to all the museums Washington had at the time. Anything historical—we were there. Lucas purchased my first car for a graduation gift. It was a blue Sprint with orange and yellow stripes down the sides.

Lucas had planned my life out for me; he wouldn't stopped

pressuring me to go into the Air Force. He had me set up to go two prep schools and Harvard University where he attended and graduated, not to forget the fact he didn't acknowledge me in the program as his child. At his graduation ceremony, he only had my brother's name and my stepmother's name listed. See, Lucas never wanted me to have kids, not even in my full adulthood. I was married and pregnant with Nicholas at sixteen years old and graduated during my seven months of pregnancy. I walked a crossed the stage with pride. Lucas and his mother Margaret attended my ceremony; they had no clue I was carrying their first grandchild and great grandchild.

During my pregnancy, I stayed away from his side of the family. Nicholas's first set of pictures was taken at two months old; this was when I decided to take him to meet his great grandmother Margaret. She held him for hours and called everyone she knew; she was a proud great grandmother. Margaret was so proud, she didn't think about asking any questions. She just held Nicholas and cried. On the other hand, when she called Lucas, he came down at his first convenience and took the Sprint back from me. He has always hated and been jealous of my son Nicholas Charron Ceasar. Lucas and his siblings hated the fact their mother did things for Nicholas and me that she was not able to do for them in their childhood years. Nicholas grew to become a brilliant young man; he graduated from Fayetteville State University with BA degree in political science with honors magna cum laude.

Nicholas was accepted at Harvard University where Lucas received his degree. Upon completing his enrollment, my dear son needed two letters of recommendation. His grandmother Dr. Margaret wrote one letter, and his grandfather Lucas refused to write the other letter. I witnessed my son experience emotional abuse and rejection as I still experience with Lucas. Nicholas looked at Lucas as his hero, his world, his dad, and the best grandfather ever. Lucas always shot him down; he would never once tell my son he was proud of him. Instead he hurt his feelings.

Shortly after Nicholas graduated from Fayetteville State University, Lucas came down. We were in my grandmother Margaret's kitchen.

Lucas asked Nicholas, "What are your plans now that you're finished with college?"

Nick's response was "I'm taking a break for about six months, and then I'm going to law school. I've started my own cleaning business, Nice & Neat Cleaning Company."

Lucas said, "You may as well forget going to law school. You're going to be too old. You need to get an eight to five job!"

Nick said, "I'm not too old!" Nick continued to say, "In my first thirty days of Nice & Neat being opened, we made over $5,000."

Lucas said, "That's no money. You should've made $20,000 to $30,000. What you made is nothing to be proud of."

I'm standing there looking at Lucas like, *You are one cold-hearted ass man. I've never seen anyone like you in my life!*

No one knows how many days and times my son would call me or come to me hurt, wanting his grandfather to be proud of him for once. Nicholas would always say, "Ma, all I want is for my grandfather Lucas to be proud of me, and he won't ever tell me no matter what I do! Why, Ma?"

I would say, "Son, it doesn't matter if he is or not. I am and your grandmother Margaret is too. We are very proud of you. Please stop worrying yourself with that. You're going have a stroke!" I said, "That's how he is, and you're going to have to accept it!"

My son ended up seeing a psychiatrist as I did; the things he was battling with in his head with his grandfather Lucas began to be overwhelming for him. A week and half before he was killed, Lucas belittled my son in a way like never before. My son Nicholas called me sobbing so bad; I began to have chest pains to hear a thirty-one-year-old man in pain because of someone he admired all his life continually hurt and belittle him to no end.

He could never get his birth father to have a relationship with him at all. He would call Wilson for things; he would lie to his son or wouldn't answer the phone or call him back. Neither Lucas nor Wilson came to Nicholas's high school graduation or college graduation, and these are the men who were supposed to have been in his life. I would always look at my son and say, "You're strong I don't know how you manage to maintain all these honors and keep your grades up and write your papers and a whole slew of other people's papers for them and still function, and you have two dysfunctional-ass people who keep you stressed the most."

The people in the world wonder why this was that way with Nick. Why did he do this and that? Let me be the one to let y'all know my son was going through the same hell I was, if not worse as I was, because of two callous people.

The same two callous people didn't even come to his funeral service, so that told a lot! Through the years, my umbilical cord became detached with all three of them: Laverne, Lucas, and Wilson. The only thing I can say is if I ever need a drop of blood to live, I don't want it from Lucas or Laverne, and if they need any blood, I can't help them, and if I don't ever see them another day in my life, it will be too soon. Lucas allowed his grandson Nicholas to be stranded on the side of the highway in Virginia about fifteen minutes or less from his home. The car Nicholas was driving had malfunctioning issues. He and his friend were stuck on side of the highway, and he called Lucas to come and pick them up; well, Lucas wouldn't go get them.

I had to call my brother to go and pick my son and his friend up off the side of the highway. I recall my son telling me during the time he was taking his high school graduation pictures that Lucas and his sister were there, and she said to Lucas, "Nicholas is not college material." That crushed Nicholas's heart; he never let that go until the day he died. They destroyed my son and mentally drove him to another way of life. I tried to save my son; I did everything in my power. The pain and agony they were continually causing him was beyond unbearable for him. They never had anything good to say to him at no time in his life. Nicholas was a very sensitive and self-conscious individual. Lucas's sister called him "fat" all the time and harped on him about his weight.

She came down with Lucas one time and threw out a lot of Nicholas's music he had written since he was five years old and some of his plays. My son said to me, "Ma, all my stuff was throwed all in the garage everywhere."

I sat and looked at the bag of medication my son was taking in order to stay sane because of his grandfather Lucas. It's was hurt I wouldn't want him to feel. No one knows what it's like to lose a child or to watch two of them waste away!

A Message for My Four Husbands!

Traveon Jermaine Ceasar (second son)

Nelson Jylil Barnett III (fourth son)

Tywun Jyhid Barnett (fifth son)

Narius Yrre Mcgougan (sixth son)

As long as life lasts and time past, always continue to strive to be the best you can be in life. Don't let what anyone say to you affect your mental capacity by no means. People who belittle you are the ones who wish they had the experience and opportunity in life as you do. It may be something you're experiencing or have experienced. Those individuals don't have the nerve to be who they really are or what they want to be, so they try to insult your intelligence. They are only bold in the areas of being ignorant as hell. I need for you four brothers to stick together and watch out for one another no matter what, and don't let anyone break that bond unless its God Almighty! *I love y'all!* Kisses from me!

A MESSAGE FOR MY THREE HUSBANDS IN HEAVEN!

Nicholas Charron Ceasar (first son)—August 29, 1989–September 30, 2020

Armonte Marquis Santa-Rita (third son)—November 2, 1992–January 25, 1993

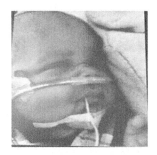

Tylilrius Charveon Stewart (seventh son)—April 24, 2013–October 17, 2013

The loss of you all has taught me that pain is different. Prior to losing any one of you, I use to think that pain was just pain. I've also learned there are different levels of feelings, emotions, pain, and mental function abilities. *I love all of you so much. My life has never been the same without you all and never will be. Continue to rest easy until Ma sees you again!*

THE MOST HATED & UNWANTED CHILD

CHARACTERS

Laverne—My mother. **"Evil-doer."** She's four feet tall with a caramel complexion and long hair. She calls herself the "Clean-up Woman." If a man is not married, she doesn't want him. She goes around deliberately harming others and making them suffer! Employed at Cross Creek Hospital as a nurse. Aka my **"Ladybug."** We were once inseparable; as the years went by things changed.

Lucas—Extremely tall with bald head. Pecan complexion. In the military, he eventually retired. Very callous individual. No bond or relations with me.

Pappy—Short with dark chocolate complexion salt and pepper hair. Retired Army Master Sgt. with purple heart. He's the only grandfather figure I ever had and close mentor to me. I could always confide in him about anything.

Margaret—Semi-medium height with a pecan tan complexion. The most beautiful brown smooth skin that's soft as cotton with a mean afro and supreme arched eyebrows, which she does herself. She looks sociably sophisticated all the times. She's Lucas mother, Boomie's grandmother, Gail's aunt, and Grace's sister. She works at College Lakes on Rosehill road in

Fayetteville, NC. She received teacher of the year award for Cumberland County schools system. She eventually retired after thirty-one years. She's the beat of my heart.

Thomas—Medium height with toffee complexion and short, wavy salt-and-pepper hair. He's a retired Marine and currently employed at the pawn shop on Bragg Blvd. Fayetteville NC. He's my godfather/sugar daddy. Our bond is inseparable.

Wilson—Short with butterscotch complexion and boxed haircut. In the United States Army. My husband and the father of Nicholas. He's from Louisiana. He's French and Creole.

Grace—Short with pecan tan complexion and beautifully supreme arched eyebrows, which she does herself, and soft curly hair. My aunt. We have an extremely close relationship. I spent weekends with her and her son. She works at the VA Medical Center on Ramsey Street Fayetteville, NC. She eventually retired after thirty-one years.

Gail—Medium height with butterscotch complexion. Big boned with wide hips, ponytail, beautifully supreme arched eyebrows, which she did herself. She's manager of a retail store. My cousin. We are extremely close. Now she's a "Bad Maama Jaama." She had the walk of a stallion!

Nelson—Tall pecan tan complexion and bald head. Works at a body shop and the city of Fayetteville. He is the father of my fourth and fifth sons. He and I are in relationship.

Loc—Tall, chocolate complexion. Long dreads and broad shoulders. He's the father of Yrre. A hustler at heart! We are in a relationship.

Yrre—He's two years old. 34.2 inches tall with low haircut and pecan tan complexion. My sixth son (Three years in Chapter 3).

Ann—She's short with a creamy butterscotch complexion,

beautiful long dreads, and a nose piercing. We are first cousins; we grew up like sisters. She just received her associates degree in recreation.

Shakeia—She's medium height with a silky cocoa chocolate complexion and long hair. My **Little sister/best friend,** she was one of my students on my school bus. She's employed at the Department of Social Service for sixteen years as of this year.

Frances—Medium height. Cocoa complexion with short curly hair, nose piercing, and piercing in both ears at the top and lower ear lobes. She works at Walmart on Ramsey Street Fayetteville, NC. Me and my aunt are close; I spent weekends with her. She is Laverne's baby sister.

Traveon—He's two months old, weighs 2 lbs. ¾ oz., and he is my third son. Short with chocolate complexion and a smile that will light up the world. He's my young buck, my third son, and little solider. He writes poems (fifteen years old in Chapter 3).

Zakar—aka **"My Bodyguard" and my best friend** of twenty-five years. Twenty-seven. She's short, thick with pecan tan complexion and beautiful medium length dreads. She's a pharmacy technician and security guard.

Nick—He's tall with cocoa chocolate complexion, medium length braids, and broad shoulders. My second husband and the father of Tylilrius. We met during my employment at KGP Logistics in Hope Mills, NC. We married January 3, 2015.

Tylilrius—He weighed 1 lb. 2 oz. at birth. Pecan tan complexion, and during the time of his passing, he weighed eleven pounds. My seventh son.

Janetta—She's medium height, fair-skinned, thick with curly hair, glasses, and drawn-on eyebrows, which she did herself. Her field of employment is daycare. She is my lover.

Bean—Short and bowlegged with low haircut. Carmel complexion, beautiful cut beard with a gold chain and locket around his neck that has my photo inside. He is the man who I considered my real father. He dated Laverne twenty years.

Paul—Tall, dark chocolate complexion with ocean waves in his low haircut with a gold wedding ring on his hand that shines bright as stars in the nighttime skies. He was married. When he walked, he twitched a time or two. He was retired from the army.

Denise—Short with cocoa complexion, finger waves in her hair, noise piercing, sliver chains and rings on all her fingers, ear piercing at the top of her ear lobes and down the side of her ears. My soul. She taught me all about the streets and how to survive, how to hold box cutter in my hand and razor blades in my mouth, and how to position my knuckles to protect myself. There is nothing she won't do for me; she's my shield.

Playboy—Short with butterscotch complexion and a gold tooth. He was a hustler at heart; he sold handbags on Murchison Road for years. He turned me on to selling the bags. He took me to New York and showed me where to go and what type of quality bags to purchase. We were already friends from times past.

Carlos—Medium height with gold tooth, long silky hair pulled back in ponytail. Stacy Adams shoes and suit. He owns a body shop, and his original home is Alabama. He's Mrs. B's husband.

Mrs. B—Short in height, perfectly round face, cocoa chocolate complexion, smooth silky skin. Coal black, silky wavy hair she wears up in a bun. Nice big, thick thighs and rump. She always has a smile on her face and her gold tooth sparkles like twinkling star. She was the manager of Carlos's body shop and his wife of twenty-five years or more. She's Nelson's mother as well as my middle two sons' grandmother. She's from Alabama.

Nicholas—Two months. 8 lbs. 7 oz. vanilla complexion, curly jet-black hair, light brown eyes, and bowlegs. He's French, Creole, and African American. **Nicholas** (Seventeen years old in Chapter 3). Tall, butterscotch complexion, light brown eyes, medium length braids straight back, and bowlegs with popping calves. He hears music in his head, and he writes the musical scores, plays the piano, and write plays. His first play was Hansel and Gretel, which they performed at Cape Fear Regional Theatre, and he starred in it. He's mixed with French, Creole, and African American.

← Ladybug   🎥   📞   🔍   ⋮

🕑 📶 42% 🔋 1:04 PM

10:54 AM

I wouldn't stay with you ever again. Don't forget you will need me before I need you. You will need me before I need you

Except I will never be here for you again.

1:04 PM

I hate you don't ever forget that

Now

⊕ 🖼   Chat message   ☺ 🎤

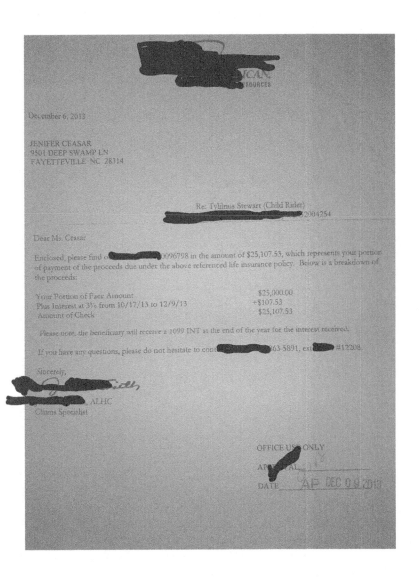

December 6, 2013

JENIFER CEASAR
9501 DEEP SWAMP LN
FAYETTEVILLE NC 28314

Re: Tylilrus Stewart (Child Rider)
2004254

Dear Ms. Ceasar:

Enclosed, please find o▮▮▮▮▮0096798 in the amount of $25,107.53, which represents your portion of payment of the proceeds due under the above referenced life insurance policy. Below is a breakdown of the proceeds:

Your Portion of Face Amount	$25,000.00
Plus Interest at 3% from 10/17/13 to 12/9/13	+$107.53
Amount of Check	$25,107.53

Please note, the beneficiary will receive a 1099 INT at the end of the year for the interest received.

If you have any questions, please do not hesitate to cont▮▮▮▮▮63-5891, ext▮▮▮ #12208.

Sincerely,

▮▮▮▮▮, ALHC
Claims Specialist

OFFICE USE ONLY

APPROVAL _____

DATE ___ AP DEC 09 2013

87

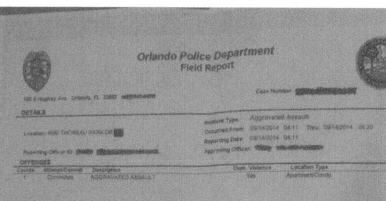

Orlando Police Department
Field Report

Case Number: [redacted]

100 S Hughey Ave, Orlando, FL 32802 [redacted]

DETAILS

Location: 4580 THOREAU PARK DR [redacted]

Reporting Officer ID: [redacted]

Incident Type: Aggravated Assault
Occurred From: 09/14/2014 04:11 Thru: 09/14/2014 04:20
Reporting Date: 09/14/2014 04:11
Approving Officer: [redacted]

OFFENSES

Counts	Attempt/Commit	Description	Dom. Violence	Location Type
1	Committed	AGGRAVATED ASSAULT	Yes	Apartment/Condo

NARRATIVE

On 09/14/2014 at 0411 hours, I Officer M. [redacted] responded to 4580 Thoreau Park Drive [redacted] (North Bridge Apartments) in reference to Threat/Assault.

Upon arrival I met with Jenifer Downing who in a sworn written statement stated she went to the park and then went to the club (Parliament House). J. Downing when she returned home to her apartment her mother, [redacted] (identified by North Carolina State Drivers' License) stated if J. Downing valued her life she would not go to sleep tonight. J. Downing stated L. [redacted] was beating on the counter with a knife, over and over. J. Downing stated she did give everyone in her family knives, to sleep with, because there have been thirteen cars broken into and eleven doors kicked recently in her apartment complex. J. Downing, however, stated that L. [redacted] does not need to walk around with a knife at all times. J. Downing stated L. [redacted] then walked over to her girlfriend (NOI) and said, "I hate you bitch". J. Downing stated she came out of a room and L. [redacted] was still in a rage and in J. Downing's face with the knife. J. Downing stated due to her mother yelling in a rage, while holding the knife, J. Downing stated she feared for her safety. J. Downing stated she felt threatened and unsafe staying in her home.

I met with Nickolas Stewart who in a sworn written statement stated, L. [redacted] is his soon-to-be mother in-law. N. Stewart is the fiance of J. Downing. N. Stewart stated L. [redacted] stated: if he valued his life, he need not be sleeping in the house tonight because he wants to see the next day. N. Stewart stated that L. [redacted] was holding a knife in her hand while she was stating this to him. N. Stewart stated he did not feel safe because J. Downing had a knife in her hand and he did not know L. [redacted] intentions. N. Stewart stated he walked outside and called the police.

Based on the above facts and circumstances probable cause was established to file charges At-Large with the State Attorney's Office on [redacted] for Aggravated Assault.

It should be noted due to L. [redacted] Transportation to The Orange County Booking and Release Center was not possible. [redacted] conducted [redacted] who approved charges being file At-Large on L. [redacted]

L. [redacted] was picked up by family members not involved in the incident and taken to The Travel Lodge (7200 International Drive).

BIOGRAPHY

Jenifer Stewart, also known as **"Boomie,"** is a first-time author. She's a unique and adventurous individual who loves to travel, sports, cooking, music, and most of all, celebrating. She has severe allergies to drama, lies, and negativity. In her lifetime, she's had seven inviolable experiences, giving *natural* birth to her seven children, who she wouldn't dream of trading for the world and would do it all again.

Mrs. Stewart is an intelligent, bold African American woman who will continue to write books to inspire individuals of the world. In her elementary years at Lucille Saunders Elementary, she was promoted early from kindergarten to first grade. Later in her high school years, she went to summer school and took eleventh grade English and math in order to skip to the twelve grade, graduating from Southview High School in 1989. She completed bank teller training in 1991, receiving her first certification. She broadened her education horizons, attending Fayetteville Technical Community College and receiving her certification in Effective Teachers Training for Substitutes and Assistants in 1997.

In 2008, she graduated with honors from FTCC, earning her diploma as an early childhood associate. In 2009, Mrs.

Stewart enrolled in University of Phoenix online in the bachelor of science health administration degree program. After a year, with just one year of courses remaining, she decided to finish her associates in general education. She worked on both of her degrees at one time. In 2010, she graduated from FTCC, making the dean's list and receiving her associates in general education.

Mrs. Stewart obtained her bachelor's of science in health administration in 2011 from the University of Phoenix. In 2015, she enrolled for a final time at FTCC in the sterile processing program and became a certified sterile processing technician.

Made in the USA
Monee, IL
23 July 2021